History and its interpretations

preface by **Marc Ferro**

Parliamentary Assembly

Council of Europe Publishing

French edition:

Histoires et interprétations

ISBN 92-871-3224-0

Edited by Sophie Jeleff, Council of Europe Publishing
Cover design: Graphic Design Workshop, Council of Europe
Cover photo: Statue of Holy Roman Emperor Ferdinand I on horseback,
by Giambologna (Giovanni da Bologna, 1529-1608), Florence

Council of Europe Publishing
F-67075 Strasbourg Cedex

ISBN 92-871-3225-9
© Council of Europe, 1997
Printed in Belgium

Founded in 1949, the Council of Europe is an intergovernmental organisation of forty member states.[1] Among its aims are: protecting and strengthening pluralist democracy and human rights, promoting the emergence of a genuine European cultural identity, seeking solutions to the problems facing society (the position of minorities, xenophobia and intolerance, environmental protection, bioethics, Aids, drugs, etc.), developing a political partnership with the new democracies of central and eastern Europe, and helping these same countries with their political, legislative and constitutional reforms.

The Committee of Ministers is the Council's decision-making body, made up of the foreign ministers of the forty member states or their permanent representatives. The consultative organ is the Parliamentary Assembly whose members are appointed by national parliaments. The Congress of Local and Regional Authorities of Europe is a consultative body representing local communities and regions.

The Parliamentary Assembly of the Council of Europe was the first European assembly to be created in the history of the continent. With delegations from forty national parliaments it is still the largest European assembly. The Assembly, which determines its own agenda, deals with current affairs and topical themes affecting society and international policy. It meets four times a year in the debating chamber of the Palais de l'Europe in plenary session open to the public. Its work has an important influence in determining the activities of the Committee of Ministers. Matters discussed by the

1. Member states of the Council of Europe (at 1 May 1997): Albania, Andorra, Austria, Belgium, Bulgaria, Croatia, Cyprus, Czech Republic, Denmark, Estonia, Finland, France, Germany, Greece, Hungary, Iceland, Ireland, Italy, Latvia, Liechtenstein, Lithuania, Luxembourg, Malta, Moldova, Netherlands, Norway, Poland, Portugal, Romania, Russian Federation, San Marino, Slovak Republic, Slovenia, Spain, Sweden, Switzerland, "the former Yugoslav Republic of Macedonia", Turkey, Ukraine, United Kingdom.

Parliamentary Assembly are also reported back by representatives to their national parliaments, and thus have an influence on governments.

History and its interpretations is based upon the report drawn up by the Parliamentary Assembly's Committee on Culture and Education on history and the learning of history in Europe (Doc. 7446, rapporteur: Mr de Puig) as well as the proceedings of the colloquy entitled: "The learning of history in Europe" (Paris, 5 and 6 December 1994).

Following a debate on the report on 22 January 1996, the Assembly adopted Recommendation 1283 on history and the learning of history in Europe, which is given in the appendix.

Contents

Preface

by Marc Ferro[1]

At the colloquy on the learning of history in Europe, many contributors expressed pessimism on the subject of the uses of history, particularly the way in which it was used as an instrument, and wondered about how it was taught and learned. How could history be taught and knowledge of it be spread in the spirit of human rights? Of course, the rapporteurs from eastern Europe were able to give an example of "historical knowledge" distorted by its dependence on an ideology encompassing the full range of social theory.

Everybody recognises the need to make history autonomous, especially those who are aware of its frequently national, if not nationalistic connotations. One might wonder whether it is possible to write a history of Europe at all, or if this history should not be seen from the outsider's point of view that is, by the peoples of former colonies, or by Americans. These questions are commonly asked, and one wonders what the content of this history might be, or what forms it could take.

One can never completely wipe out the past, and the link between that past and the present needs to be understood, if only to guard against the repetition of certain tragic events. This is also true of

---

1. Marc Ferro is a historian, co-director of *Annales*, and president of the association for research at the Ecole des hautes études en sciences sociales, Paris. Marc Ferro was the co-ordinator of the Council of Europe colloquy entitled "The learning of history in Europe" (Paris, 5 and 6 December 1994).

myths and their survival: should they be reproduced, analysed, and criticised? The same applies to "facts" that are acknowledged, constructed, or imaginary; do they not have an effect on the history that is in the process of being made? How should these facts be dealt with?

Another problem lies in the uncertainties of history, the analysis of societies and their past. The failure of ideologies, of comprehensive systems for explanation and meaning, and the use that has been made of them has proved that each system chooses its own facts, its heros, its own way of dividing up history into periods, and its methods of classification. Also, the increase in the number of history's "breeding grounds" as a result of decolonisation and the rebirth of nationalism in different areas, has created an additional variable. Finally, the discrediting of "official" history has served to enhance the value of memory, and the associated places, without it necessarily being realised that making memory sacred is also excessive, and that analysis often shows that this kind of memory is just as illusory as other kinds of history.

The result of widespread cinema viewing, and to an even greater extent, television viewing, is that most young people's knowledge of history is gained outside school with as yet poorly understood consequences. It is clear, though, that television and cinema have the effect of modifying one's vision of history more than novels or the theatre: programmes alter the chronological order of events, choose situations that are likely to please, and dramatise the telling of facts: according to a survey carried out by a Centre for Peda-gogical Research and Documentation (CRDP) in France it is this dramatisation that people remember, although it may not neces-sarily correspond to "what really happened", nor to the results of investigations.

One's knowledge of the past also depends on several variables. First, the choice of sources of information, or rather the hierarchical principle governing this choice, as some sources are considered to be of greater value than others. State archives are more highly valued than private archives; a letter written by Churchill would be taken more seriously than an anonymous account, and secret documents are judged, rightly or wrongly, to be more reliable than published documents such as press reports. This is a questionable attitude, which takes Bukharin's confessions at face value and reduces historical analysis to the reproduction of the speeches of political or economic leaders, even if this is done in a critical manner. The result is that an easily digestible "official" history is served up, or history seen through the eyes of those at the top, in which the voice of society is expressed only through those who speak on its behalf.

Historical texts are generally organised chronologically, with the dating of the text and knowledge of it remaining one of the criteria for establishing its veracity and the professionalism of the practitioners involved. They are presented in the form of narrative accounts, which reconstitute or, better still, reconstruct the past and its links with the present. However, this kind of account has the disadvantage of not justifying its choice of facts and arguments; it willingly reveals its sources but not the principle behind the secret of its manufacture. It might be suspected of succumbing to several excesses, especially rhetorical, not to mention its potential partiality. Imagine how many different versions of the French Revolution could be written using the same documents, and the same eye-witness accounts.

It was as a reaction to these modes of production and these uncertainties, that the Annales school was founded in 1929 in Strasbourg, a place where several different versions of history existed side by side: French and German, Catholic and Protestant, religious and non-religious, regionalist and national. The school was founded by Lucien Fèbvre and Marc Bloch, and its aim was to replace chronological narrative accounts with the analysis of problems, explaining one's choice of documentation, justifying one's working method, and giving priority to working out a method of analysis, modelled on procedure in the social sciences or sociology, economics, experimental medicine, or geography.

Over the last few decades, some of these principles have been incorporated into history-teaching methods in order to boost the autonomy of the subject, and to improve the understanding of the relationship between known facts, family, data on work, the environment, and so on, and the outside world. However, by questioning all non-constructed knowledge, this method of teaching has the effect of stripping subjects of their cultural context and removing them from the collective memory, from one's knowledge of a past which, although perhaps not authenticated, functions nevertheless as an agent of history in that it moulds attitudes.

Several suggestions were made during the colloquy on "The teaching of history in Europe" for redesigning history teaching on the basis of several criteria: chronology, continuity and disruptions, slow change, awareness of the extent and topicality of phenomena, and so on. But emphasis was also placed on the need to improve the management of the audiovisual media for history-teaching purposes, and not to allow image professionals to think they could set themselves up as historians. As for the rest, it has become increasingly difficult on television to impose a consistent and voluntarist vision of history, as the job of recounting and interpreting history is slipping from the grasp of its traditional agents: historians, writers and politicians. This may have sometimes resulted in the worst excesses (as in Romania and the Gulf war, for example), but it has also brought about – and television has helped here – the removal of numerous taboos buried deep in traditional institutions.

It remains for us to list the different places and institutions where societies' collective memory and knowledge take shape and develop. Firstly, textbooks, which, paradoxically, all the participants in the colloquy were busy examining and criticising, although they admitted themselves that adolescents obtained most of their knowledge from other sources. Television and cinema were also mentioned, but museums, where the visitor is relatively free to move and look around (which accounts for their current revival) should not be forgotten. Similarly, visiting towns or castles has the advantage of showing different stages in history, instead of just displaying similar exhibits (paintings, furniture, and so on) in different rooms. The need to combine all these sources of knowledge was emphasised, yet these sources are not governed by the same principles of classification. They reflect the principles of the state in the press (political or economic events, for example), those of the sciences in universities (according to discipline) and the different types of programmes on television (news, short features, documentary dramas, fiction).

Knowledge of audiovisual texts must be created or developed as a matter of urgency, as well as the ability to read and decode them, and integrate them into more general knowledge gained from other sources of history.

Thought should be given to producing a history of Europe which, in one way or another, takes into account the collective memory of societies (such as minorities and outcasts), not forgetting to include the different taboos and prohibitions and analyse them, together with "revisionist" theories (seeking for example to deny the existence of the gas chambers, the massacres in Armenia, and the tragedies of Africa) which can then be properly denounced. Cooperation on an international level is called for, which does not necessarily imply international drafting.

The exclusive use of one form of history learning, such as visiting museums, reading textbooks or watching television, should be discouraged, and learning to combine these forms encouraged.

History should not serve a state or an ideology, it should help in the protection of human rights and citizen's rights. To this end, historians should be given protection, and the Council of Europe should help provide this protection.

Introduction

History as we learnt it at school and university represents only a part of our historical knowledge. History is also learnt outside the education system, and very often we pick up bits and pieces of history from political life, literature or art. It is not only professional historians who can tell us about history.

The concept of history teaching should therefore be expanded into the wider, more comprehensive concept of history learning. It is a concept covering all the historical knowledge a citizen acquires in the course of their education and life. On that basis we may consider what kind of history is learnt, how it is learnt and why.

Over and beyond problems specific to the teaching of history, the treatment of history by television, which is a historical document in itself, should be taken into consideration. This involves seeing how history is treated in newspapers and magazines, on radio, in museums and by the cinema (both as a historical document and an interpretation of history) as well as in political discussions.

The debate is not about the history of Europe, but about history in Europe. It is impossible to write a single European history because one comes up against different interpretations, contrasting ideas and probably insurmountable methodological and ideological disagreements. And it is only right that this should be so, otherwise history would be dogmatic. If the choice lay between dogmatic or pluralistic history, it would be better to opt for the latter.

In an information society the diversity of sources of historical evaluation is becoming increasingly obvious. Moreover, the concern to encourage tolerance and acceptance of others has intensified. Thus, the Council of Europe wishes to embark on a further process of thinking with a view to reminding governments and public opinion how important, indeed fundamental, history learning is. We can no longer accept that history as it is taught today and tomorrow should be false, manipulated or trivialised.

In the present European context it is increasingly necessary to denounce manipulations of history, the frivolous and superficial way in which history is often treated and, of course, the exploitation of history for obnoxious causes, as is being done in the Balkans.

NB: the introductory texts to each section have been taken from the report on history and the learning of history in Europe (Doc. 7446) drawn up by Mr de Puig on behalf of the Parliamentary Assembly's Committee on Culture and Education.

Politics and history

History has an inescapable function of enhancement, judgment, contrast and reference. We look at the past with our present-day mentality, our own problems, our own view of the world and of society and our own ideas. That is why the interpretation of each historical period contains new meanings. An aseptic, timeless history unrelated to our immediate present would be nothing more than a literary exercise. History concerns our present, and we should be aware of this.

Although the role of history may be regarded as a minor problem, it is a priority matter in view of history's direct relationship with ideology, nationalism, tolerance (or intolerance), racism (or anti-racism), social attitudes and, in general, a society's forms of understanding and functioning.

History is therefore a political issue. Any investigation or analysis of the past is naturally conditioned by the historian, who will declare as positive anything that is positive in her/his own opinion. The very choice of topics, sources, methods and bibliography involves subjective, ideological and political elements. Here lies one of the primary political factors of history : the political awareness of the person studying it.

The use of history is not in itself negative. History renders, and has always rendered, considerable services to the progress of human-ity. Historical experience, a knowledge of the past, the collective memory, the evaluation of previous successes and mistakes, the heritage bequeathed to us by past ages, humanity's progress, its technological, cultural, humanistic and social achievements – all this influences politics, and therefore history has often been the weapon and emblem of positive movements and changes. History invests politics with arguments and reasons. It can legitimise politics provided that it is not misused and does not serve despotic, antidemocratic or antisocial interests.

Consequently, it is legitimate to make use of history and historical references in politics if two criteria are met;

– what is used must really be history, that is, we should be capable of adopting a critical approach to the analysis of historical facts and any possible interpretations. We should proceed from history to politics, not vice versa, as the usual process is that on the basis of a political proposition one tries to find historical references, whether relevant or not, whether reliable and consistent or not;

– history should be used for worthy and just causes. It is so vast, diverse and terrible that it can provide all kinds of examples for unscrupulous people. The worst horrors, wars, dominations, authoritarianism and exploitations of humanity have been justified by means of theories and arguments deriving from historical facts. It is unacceptable to resort to history for the purpose of building an unjust future.

If some examples needed to be given of the legitimate use of history, it would be sufficient to point out how widespread the principles underlying the French Revolution have become or to refer to the nazi regime and the Holocaust as the kinds of aberrations that should be avoided in future. On the other hand, one only has to observe how history is being used by the National Front in France to realise that here is an example of a perverse interpretation of history. Let us not forget either the gigantic manipulation of history by the Soviet regime, which succeeded not only in inventing a history consistent with its doctrinal postulates but also, by dogmatising theories of Hegel and Marx, in creating the "infallible" method of historical analysis and squandering the fundamental contribution of historical materialism, transformed it into an instrument of a political doctrine which, by definition, it had to serve.

The two main trends in the use and misuse of history for political purposes have been concentrated on the national question or the social question: in the first instance, for the identification of the group or the emancipation of man; then, as national or social history which, in its extreme or extremist forms, has been patriotic – and even chauvinistic – history and revolutionary or reactionary history.

There is nothing reprehensible about the fact that peoples seek signs of their identity in history, especially as it is obvious that a national human community has necessarily been created through a historical process of a specific and individual kind. The national history of each people thus has a meaning of its own. The same is not true of nationalistic or chauvinistic history, which aspires not to explain the national characteristics of a group but to create nationalistic attitudes by means of indoctrination against external enemies. Whereas national history is an element inherent in the human condition, in the identification of the individual with his own group, in the very existence of the nation and in the discourse of world history, history of a nationalistic and patriotic kind, on the other hand, fosters confrontation and exclusion. It seeks to subject the whole future to the mythical idea of the nation, while justifying everything in this way.

The same applies to the social question. It is quite logical and even desirable that a critical history should be an instrument of emancipation for individuals and social classes. Historical analysis has undoubtedly made a decisive contribution in the past to remedying injustices, exploitation, slavery and subservience. The concepts of freedom, democracy, equality, social justice and solidarity, as well as their advancement, are – although limited and precarious – partly due to historical experience. History harbours the seed of social progress, as it shows what should change and be altered if man is to live in fairer and more equitable conditions. Accordingly, history is a catalyst of social change and of human and humanistic progress.

However, its use as an instrument of revolution, that is of radical transformation or sudden acceleration of historical processes, has not always been accompanied by rigour and circumspection. Sometimes historical analysis and its forced, manipulated theories have served as a pretext for changes that have been retrograde rather than progressive.

National history and nationalist history

No one can deny a national community's right to its history. The very existence of a group presupposes a historical evolution that determines its cohesion. It is therefore normal that each nation should have a national history and that historical awareness should underlie national political awareness. A coherent explanation – whether triumphant or tragic – of the nation's continuity becomes a patriotic necessity.

A problem arises when we move from national history to national-istic history, as very often happens. History is then used for propaganda and indoctrination purposes. Whereas national history seeks unifying elements to explain its existence, nationalistic history tries to justify patriotic values by exacerbating epic and mythical aspects and "national" characteristics. It emphasises differences in relation to neighbouring countries, exalts uniformity, conceals the history of regions and minorities and always defines itself in relation to external enemies. It is the cause of ethnic conflicts. The case of the former Yugoslavia is a telling example. In Serb and Croat history textbooks the "historical" descriptions are totally distorted by the nationalistic spirit.

In Europe, the dominant idea since the nineteenth century has been that a nation should be compact, uniform, monocultural, monolinguistic, standardised, equalised and centralised. To support this concept, it was necessary to produce a compact, uniform, monocultural history. Differences, diversities, external influences and crossbreeding were therefore denied. And yet the history of our countries is basically diverse, pluricultural and pluri-ethnic, with external influences that are so decisive that it is sometimes difficult to tell whether more is owed to "foreigners" or to nationals.

History of Europe

Europe is the history of an immense accumulation of diversities, a blend of ideas and races. Under the colours of national histories there emerges a Europe that is more mixed and uniform than the one we were told about. It is not homogeneous, but it has many shared elements, including a largely common history.

There is no single history of Europe, even though Europe's past was necessarily single. The existence of many books entitled *History of Europe* shows that there is a multiplicity of interpretations of facts. What one country may cherish as a positive, even glorious memory (a military victory, the achievement of independence) may be regarded as a disaster by a neighbouring country. The past was what it was, and its enhancement no doubt depends on the present. It is wrong to manipulate history, but it is not necessary to have only one view of the past either.

On the other hand, if Europe exists as a differentiated, identifiable reality, if there is a global conception of Europe, it should be possible to write the history of that reality, of its origins and contradictions, of the various kinds of experiences that led up to the present-day plan for Europe's integration.

We should not lose hope but try to foster a coherent explanation of our past. To begin with, we might study how a chapter containing the generally accepted basic facts about the various histories of Europe's peoples might be incorporated in all European history textbooks. Then, after thorough investigations, it might be possible to write a history of Europe that is not completely contemptible.

History in central and eastern Europe

Although there has been talk of manipulations of history in western Europe, this bears no comparison with what has happened in the countries of central and eastern Europe. The dogmatic political tendentiousness of history teaching has left these countries faced with the urgent and difficult necessity of rediscovering their true history.

They need history textbooks, retraining courses for teachers, new research methods and reformed educational plans and systems. The need is urgent, as the dissemination of a critical, rigorous history can help those countries to recapture their true identities, without lapsing into some other dogmatism.

The totalitarian systems of this part of Europe manipulated history to such an extent that it will take decades to restore historical normality. It is important to rehabilitate the history flouted by the Soviet regime, together with the various symbols, artistic works, books, archives, libraries and names of things, streets, cities and places. This has also been observed in the Baltic states.

In this connection it is worth mentioning the *Black book on the heinous extermination of Jews by the German fascist invaders in the temporarily occupied regions of the USSR and in the*

camps in Poland during the 1941-45 war.[1] At the time of the
invasion of the Soviet Union by Hitler's armies in 1941, Stalin supported the creation of a Jewish antifascist committee with a view to
mobilising world opinion. At the suggestion of Albert Einstein,
some members of the committee wrote the *Black book* on the
basis of the accounts, notes and diaries of survivors, witnesses or
torturers. However, priorities changed and the book was never
published. First of all, Stalin ordered the removal of references to
participation by Ukrainians, Lithuanians, Russians and others in
nazi crimes; then he ordered the deletion of accounts concerning
the Jewish resistance in the ghettos "to avoid encouraging Jewish
nationalism". In 1947 the book was banned when it was about to
be printed as it contained "serious political errors". The chairman
of the Jewish antifascist committee was murdered in 1948, and
some of its members, including several of the authors of the *Black
book*, were arrested, tortured, convicted and executed in 1952. In
1989 the original version of the *Black book* was discovered in the
archives of the KGB, but it was not until 1993 that the book was
finally published in Russian in Vilnius.

Problems of place-names

Alongside the linguistic evolution that resulted in the town of
Caesar Augusta being transformed into Saragossa and Djebel Tariq
into Gibraltar, historical upheavals often lead to changes in place
names. Thus the city of Byzantium became Constantinople in the
fourth century, then Istanbul as from the fifteenth century, while
the city which the Germans called Pressburg in the Middle Ages
was the capital of Hungary for more more than 300 years with the
name Poszonyi and is today the capital of Slovakia with the name
Bratislava. There are also cities which, after two or three changes,

1. This paragraph is based on an article by Annette Lévy Willard which
appeared in the French newspaper *Libération* on 16 November 1995.

revert to their former or original names. This was the case, for example, with Chemnitz to Karl-Marx-Stadt back to Chemnitz and with St Petersburg to Petrograd to Leningrad back to St Petersburg.

These place-name changes, even though not always peaceful, have been the consequence of historical modifications. Above all (but not only) in central and eastern Europe, one also often comes across towns and villages that have two or three different names, even though only one name is official. Usually it is the same name in different languages, owing to a mixed population, as is the case with Nicosia/Lefkosa in Cyprus and/or to border changes, as is the case with Caporetto/Karfeit/Kobarid in Slovenia.

There is also the particular instance of the Baltic region once inhabited by Prussians. Wedged between the Lithuanians and the Poles, it was conquered in the thirteenth century by the Teuton knights, decimated by plague in 1709, heavily Germanised by Bismarck in the nineteenth century and, finally, systematically Russified by the Soviet Union after 1945. This last "operation" removed from the map of Europe a people that had itself already disappeared as a result of amalgamation with the Lithuanians, Poles and Germans, but whose memory remained in the toponymics and hydronymics of the region it had inhabited.[1]

History often repeats itself, but it never goes backwards, and decisions in this matter should lie in the first instance with the populations concerned.

---

1. See the Council of Europe's European Charter for Regional or Minority Languages which, in paragraph 2.g of Article 10 seeks to encourage "the use or adoption, if necessary in conjunction with the name in the official language(s), of traditional and correct forms of place-names in regional or minority languages", even [or especially?] if these are no longer spoken.

RUSSIA'S ETERNAL RECURRENCE

by Yuri Afanasyev[1]

As far as Russia is concerned, the question of history as a science is complicated and even dramatic. It is not only a matter of the specific, unusual and even unique way of social development of Russia. History teaching can be considered as a specific problem because the history of the Soviet period constitutes eighty years ; in addition, this great experiment that lasted for eighty years had a negative result. Teachers when explaining this period to their students must be aware of this negative and in a sense even tragic outcome.

But this is not the only aspect that is complicated and unique in the work of history teachers. We must also take into consideration that before 1917 we were always trying to reach somebody else's level of attainment. Probably since the time of Ivan the Terrible, or at least since the time of Peter I, our historical role models were conquerors.

Few would deny that present-day Russian society is a society in transition. We normally run into difficulty when we try to say what kind of transformation it is. No one doubts that it is a transition from socialism to post-socialism. At the same time, however, it is a transformation from traditionalism into liberalism, although this point of view is not supported by many historians. To my mind the main feature of this period is the process of change from traditional to modern values. Only this may give the process of reform in Russia any really positive results.

---

1. This speech was written for the colloquy "The learning of history in Europe" (Paris, 1994). Yuri Afanasyev is director of the Russian Humanistic University of Moscow.

The problem of traditionalism in Russian society is that its predominant notion is of collectivity and not of the individual. That means that the individual is not seen as the basis of an economically free society. Transition from this traditionalism into modern society creates not only a new social and economic system, but a new type of culture.

At the end of the nineteenth and beginning of the twentieth century this transition was widely discussed by Russian philosophers and writers, who compared Russia with centaurs in order to illustrate the dualism and the binary structure of Russian culture.

The way I have described things is very schematic, but if pupils and students are taught that nothing in our past was satisfactory, it could lead to the question: if our history is not a normal one, if it is uncertain, who are we? If the problem is stated in this way it will turn everything into dark, negative and problematic colours.

At the same time it is true that this binary nature of Russian culture contains not only problems and contradictions, but also serves as a sort of programmed capacity to accept alternatives, to choose between different directions of progress. However, when it became clear that the unusual and artificial historical development of the last eighty years was not working out, it was also obvious that the problem was affecting not only the sphere of education but also that of society.

There is another aspect to this problem. This is not precisely the story of those who study, but rather that of our politicians. Our society is currently going through a period of transformation, a stage of fundamental reforms. We must ask ourselves how Russian history might help us to carry out successfully these reforms in Russia today.

Russian history has already been through a period of reformation when several positive things were done. This was the period of the great reforms of the middle of the nineteenth century with such personalities as Alexander II, Stolypin and Witte. But even those reforms that were seriously formulated and took Russian traditions into account ended in disaster – by that I mean the disaster of 1917.

The present-day reformers are in a more complicated situation because they seem to turn a deaf ear to the experience of the whole of Russian history. For example, our Prime Minister Tchernomyrdin proposed the following programme for the immediate future:

– 1995: the year of financial stabilisation;

– 1996: the depression is overcome and conditions for economic recovery are created; stable economic growth is achieved;

– 1997: the beginning of regular economic growth.

This kind of programme would only lead Russian society and the rest of the world to create a new set of lies as there is no basis in our past or in our present for any such expectations.

If we consider the economic sector, we will find that the economy that was set up in the Soviet era has no possibilities to develop or to change by itself. It is controlled by the military and by heavy and basic industries. This sector is composed of giant enterprises and enormous complexes.

Here are a few examples: in 1989 87% of heavy industrial goods were produced by monopoly enterprises. Now there are 2 500 such enterprises – 80% of their production is destined for the army and not the private consumer.

These enterprises determine the functioning of the whole of industry and transport. They play no part in free market exchange and cannot be integrated into it. In this context if we look at the statement of the prime minister about stabilisation and economic growth in 1997, we should ask what kind of stabilisation he is referring to. The structure of military production, hypercentralised and based on the principle of administrative distribution, has no real possibilities of natural development and can only work with the help of non-economic instruments and forced distribution of funds.

If we examine this problem more generally, we should ask ourselves the following question. Is it possible to reform the economic system and society as a whole while maintaining Russia as a superpower and predominant, if not in the whole world, at least in the sphere of its present interests? This sphere includes central and eastern Europe. This is not my point of view, but that of those who declare it. We should point out that this sphere includes, of course, the former Soviet republics.

In 1994, the Russian Government declared that it was turning from evolutionary reform to one of "shock therapy".

The president himself has rejected populism and expressed his support for fundamental economic reforms. It is symptomatic that the declaration of progress towards economic reform and democracy coincided with the aggression against Chechnya, involving great military efforts. All these projects together with such aggressive militarist behaviour show, as in previous periods, that the authorities and rulers of Russia have not taken our history seriously. This makes their policy unpredictable. This can be clearly seen in the position of our Minister of Foreign Affairs, Kozyrev. Though it is not stated out loud, this policy is still based on perfidy and force.

In order to avoid this, there is no other possibility than to take into consideration the experience of history and integrate it into present policy. There is no other way to make policy-making democratic.

From a long-term point of view, Russian society provides a particularly interesting example in defining the different types of social and economic dynamics in history.

To give an example of some of the most well known types of development, there are "inert" societies, followed by those with an *ancien régime* type of economic development, then those which have taken off to become societies with a growth economy, and finally, those characterised by different types of post-industrial development.

Russia is a special case, however, and its own particular dynamic does not fit into any of these categories. It is all the more interesting in that it is not purely theoretical, as the existence of different types of social dynamic is giving rise to planetary contradictions, crises and dangers in today's world.

Merely listing the most well-known dangers emanating from Russia is frightening:

– conflicts and wars between ethnic groups (Chechens – Transcaucasia/central Asia);

– crime: 2 500 societies for organised crime exist in Russia today, forming 150 larger groups;

– accidents and disasters: in 1993 there were 923 fatal accidents, in which 1 050 people were killed, and during the first five months of 1994 there were 811 victims of 489 accidents. In addition to this, 40 million people live in areas that are ecologically at risk;

– the dilapidated state of industrial equipment, communications and transport: 60% of the equipment is worn out and has not been replaced for thirty years.

These are the consequences of socialist rule. However, there are also other more deep-seated reasons, which have their roots not only in the Soviet years but also in earlier centuries of Russian history. One specific point to be underlined is that the Soviet era did not abolish or erase everything that existed before 1917. On the contrary, it accentuated and reinforced the centuries-old features of the Russian social dynamic. What are these features?

More than 150 years ago, the Russian philosopher Pyotr Chaadeyev wrote that the Russians were a lost people, wandering aimlessly through history, in other words in movement, but with no progression and no development. This is a phenomenon of an "end without a beginning" which is inevitably leading Russia into deadlock and collapse. This unfortunate phenomenon of non-development is at the heart of Russia's destiny.

What facts today confirm this? First of all, the social foundations of Russia and its changes, not only in terms of its economy, laws and value system, but also the question of Russia's identity and that of an age-old way of life, passed down through forty generations, which features community life, choral singing, and *sobornost*, or "togetherness". Russian society is in a state of transition. Private or state ownership? Individualism or collectivism? Free competition or monopolies? Who knows? Everything is in a state of confusion. I do not mean confusion in the sense of "a lack of clarity", but rather, confusion in the sense of "which of these choices will prevail? A prerequisite for answering this kind of question is the reality of each of the factors involved in the choice. For the moment it is difficult to say with any certainty whether, in Russian society, all these tendencies will be present, equally, as forces able to compete with each other.

Even more concretely, during the Stolypin land reform (1907-15), 2,5 million individual farms were set up on land which was previously collectively owned by the village communes. These holdings accounted for 27% of the total number of farms in 1916, yet it cannot be said that the Stolypin reforms were a success. The reason for this is that, although the figure seems high even by today's standards, the reforms failed to diminish the importance and strength of the village communes.

Traditionalism and *sobornost* prevailed: of the 135 000 farming communities in European Russia in 1905, there were still 110 000 in 1917. After the failure of the Stolypin reforms, everything that was privately and individually owned in the Russian countryside for about eighty years was economically, physically and ideologically destroyed. As a result, 27 000 *kolkhozes* and *sovkhozes* still have their foundations in Russian traditionalism.

In the last five years about 270 000 farms have been created. Today their number is decreasing. The last farming community reform was abandoned.

One more figure, if you will forgive me. No more than 9% of the 222 million hectares of cultivable land belongs to private farms.

The transition from community to individualism has also been slow to start in towns. The *agroprom*, or agro-industry, has been replaced by the military-industrial complex and the *kolkhoze* by the factory collective. But socially it is the same as before: collectivism but no individualism.

Russia has tried several times to break this circle of non-development; it tried to find a linear form of social dynamic, and to follow the European, or capitalist, path. Each time without success. There was Peter the Great, Alexander II, Witte and Stolypin, and the Bolsheviks, followed by today's democratic reformers, who have put capitalism back on the agenda. Each time these attempts have resulted in either reinforcement of the lack of freedom or, again, in non-development. Yet again, why is this? For me, the answer lies in the attempts by all the Russian reformers over the centuries to reconcile what is irreconcilable: releasing Russia's internal forces, yet at the same time remaining a great power. It is for this reason that, in Russia, this type of movement has taken hold; people feel they must try to catch up with those ahead, conquer, and spread outwards, building artificial edifices which prevent independent self-development.

This process of construction goes by many different names: the Russian empire, a socialist society, a totalitarian regime, and, why not, democratic Russia.

Is there any way out of this vicious circle? What are the alternatives? To refuse the ideology and politics of a great power, which means transforming economic structures accordingly, not for the purposes of war but for the good of the people, something which has never been done in Russia's entire history? To grant more autonomy and freedom to the regions, not levelling down or stifling them but letting them breathe, and finally starting to build a federation, or a particular type of confederation? To shift the focus of political stability from external actions which are of no benefit to Russia to the constant encouragement of internal reform?

However desirable these strategies may seem, they are almost utopian. In reality, the opposite is happening and the same old circle continues: fulfilling the corporative interests of the military-industrial complex, *agroprom*, bureaucracy and the financing of profiteers.

THE USES OF HISTORY

by Joaquim Nadal i Farreras[1]

Anyone who works in the social sciences field, whether exclusively in teaching or combining teaching and research, may often be assailed by doubts of all kinds. In a largely pragmatic society dominated by utilitarian concepts it is not easy to find a plausible use for history.

Teachers and students of history alike have difficulty answering the question : what use is history ? A large proportion of the population would be unable to give a coherent and convincing answer to the question. An inability to come up with an explicit reply, however, does not mean that there is not an undeniable sense of history, a decisive need for history, an urgent need to have and to dominate a historical debate in specific fields and evidence of tacit "consumption" of history by the majority of the population. Synchronic and atemporal visions of the world lack both significance and impact, giving the impression that humankind is devoid of character, profile and shape. Hence any aseptic, descriptive, narrative approach from a distance, in laboratory style, leads only to a tired, bored and indifferent reaction.

A strictly academic approach to history, claiming to be neutral, merely becomes an instrument for the mechanical reproduction and transmission of a given amount of knowledge, the only benefit of which is that it guarantees that the same old facts are communicated and protected from alteration. With all the trouble it involves, this linear and limited approach is not the key to instilling a modicum of cultural background knowledge enabling people to

1. This speech was written for the colloquy "The learning of history in Europe" (Paris, 1994). Joaquin Nadal i Farreras is professor of contemporary history at Girona University and Mayor of Girona.

benefit from reading the newspaper. Narrow presentations of facts have no interest, stifling people's historical awareness. They make people lethargic and send them to sleep. And it is possible that historians go beyond their historical awareness as they define specific projects in the broadest possible terms, intending to achieve precisely that effect, aiming for that result. It is superfluous to state, in addition, that it is also possible to take a less devious view of these tendencies and simply justify these debates as being the easiest way of maintaining and perpetuating an insignificant academic purpose.

It is still possible, at the other extreme, to find doctrinaire, catechistic tendencies, of dogmatic simplicity, almost "by order", operational schemes for providing mechanical responses to absolutely any situation. Attempts to indoctrinate explicitly acknowledge at least that history has some degree of usefulness. Perverted to their maximum extent, these schemes would provide absolute justification for forcibly imposed and aprioristic ideas. These positions are not free from a certain redemptorist attitude, from the use of history as a pretext and as a vehicle to justify effectively imposing ideas and theories based upon the deprivation of elementary and fundamental rights. Rights both individual and collective.

In this field, too, history cannot really arouse much passion. Classes have their fill of plenty of other visions, their stupefied and distant brains incapable of taking in the travel offered to them. Thus scepticism spreads, the character of individuals and community alike is diminished, and the ultimate outcome is rebellion pure and simple in the face of such obviously meaningless material.

There is only one operational means, involving diverse and complex methods, of putting an end to this suffocating and self-destroying process. The use of considered debate. A contribution from a critical viewpoint, helping people to understand the motives and reasons for events and, in particular, for action, how and why they were as they were. Going beyond individuality and stimulating an ability to analyse the behaviour of society. Knowing how to ascertain who the members of a group are, and who it is that takes any given group in one direction or another. This is precisely the point at which the fundamental difficulty and essential attraction of history learning lie. Discovering, or helping others to discover, why society acted as it did is an undertaking on such a scale, having such a dimension, that enthusiasm and passion may be aroused. But it is by no means easy to achieve this in the sphere of education. Those who succeed find it not at all easy to maintain the necessary tone, keep their guard up and guarantee the methodological and ideological tension that a historical debate of this kind requires. Many of us have succumbed during our attempts, grown weary in the face of the constant contradiction between methodological expectations, ideological assumptions and results achieved, and sought alternative paths.

Politics offers history a splendid field for testing the uses and abuses of history, the possibilities and perversions of the historical debate. I view this from two angles. Firstly as a historian with a political role to play, having drawn from my basic historical training the main elements for practical action in the political field. And secondly as a politician amazed to have to live with the simplifications, equivocations, manipulations, deviations and contradictions to which an irrepressible crowd of politicians resort when referring to history.

I placed a local subject, a very specific locality, namely a single city, under my historian's microscope. One city within its country and its surroundings, of course, but I did restrict myself quite clearly to that city. That may seem a parochial, provincial, limited approach. But my political approach upon the basis of history was intended to achieve exactly the opposite effect. The intention was to carry out an ongoing and critical review of the history of the city. A review, first and foremost, of the ideological debate inspired by all the historiographic visions of it. The spider's web had to be removed, the pitfalls eliminated, the overlying concepts separated and the relationships within society and the city's consequent advances and retreats analysed from a different angle.

My city is a captive of history, trapped in its official history. The resulting single, unilateral view of its history has played a deterministic role from the viewpoint of both present and future. The future was a response to that past. Any future not reflected in its entirety in the past was a betrayal, a departure from the natural qualities and the soul of the city. It was not, however, difficult to put a halt to this tendency, which bore too heavy a burden of paralysing will, a will to go on in the same, sterile manner, an ominous acceptance of disasters and limitations, an exaltation of suicidal acts of heroism, a transformation into myth of the most destructive incidents throughout the locality. I used my own historical baggage to prepare a vision of, an all-embracing approach to, the complex social fabric of the city. How many material (physical) and social (human) realities remained hidden within the academic, media, social and official views of the city? How many neighbourhoods were unfamiliar to us, and how many were unknown to the centre, the historic centre of the city? Such a limited and inaccurate view of a broad reality! Even now, fifteen years (and four re-elections) later, I can report that my political opponents from similar social origins to my own (by which I mean from the same class), but holding different ideas, are still amazed that they lost elections they assumed they would win easily. They were ignorant of the city's history and were unwilling to dissect it precisely and thoroughly. They were blinkered by their vision of the community's history as its inheritance, an exclusive view of society, a sectarian tendency in the face of reality.

Nevertheless, I do not wish this contribution of mine to be thought of as a pedantic exaltation of history and of the use (usefulness) of a historical vision in the political sphere; I myself found it easy to quote history and did my audience's thinking for it when I converted the minor, insignificant episode of the year 785 (the submission of the citizens of Girona to Charlemagne) into the 1 200 pompous years of a European mission. A real occurrence served as the basis for a fine, politically useful fantasy.

This is where we come to the vague, fatal meeting point of the use, misuse and abuse of history.

Most of the commemorations fuelling myths, diluting analysis and giving interpretations an official status correspond to what we might call misuse of history. This misuse is cyclical and has immediate effect. Utilitarian, it functions briefly. But it is so transparently mis-used that it seems possible that it may almost be innocuous. The use of history as an instrument is so obvious, so commonplace, so limited, that it becomes a part of folklore, doing very little harm. Anything which harms history also harms politics. Politics and politicians are searching for roots and justification, they project aspirations towards the past, move with impunity across frontiers and draw on contradictory sources. Anything goes, even if it inter-rupts the coherence of a more general debate. In Catalonia, for example, it is said that a national vision is being affirmed on the basis of a mythical claim to the glories and splendour of Mediter-ranean expansion (a country with its own state), or on that of the assertion of slavishly imitated political models of that splendour during the sixteenth and seventeenth centuries, with no mention of its agonies, its oligarchical nature and the rigidity that may result. This makes it easier to claim without embarrassment the economic achievements of Charles III at the height of the Bourbon period of centralisation. Hence simultaneous commemorations of Charles III's bicentenary based upon different viewpoints in Spain and Catalonia. Our 1992 ceremonies and the 1789 celebrations in France would give rise to similar interpretations, which could lead to affirmations ranging from self-satisfaction to imbecility to national pedantry.

Abuse, with all its virulence, is present in more subtle areas. By which I mean less openly affirmed: it is when history is used as a pretext to justify the subordination or subsidiarity of people and territories, when rights are affirmed only at the expense of others' rights, or when we absurdly attempt to build new and/or important political edifices, with reference solely to history – a historical vision usually tailor-made, not for the makers or recorders of history, but for those who make use of it and mock the values of culture, civilisation and the sacredness of collective freedoms.

On the learning of history

An analysis of the factors contributing to the perception of history shows that the leading one is the teaching of history in schools. Then, by way of not insignificant complementary factors, come the historical concepts transmitted by the media (printed and audio-visual), literature, cinema and museums. Next come the influences of religion, politicians, local communities, personal contacts, and so on, which may increase, contradict or supplement knowledge acquired in the classroom.

The learning of history is a diversified process: individual reconstruction of the past; visits to museums or castles; mass media; comparison of personal experience with observations made by others.

A research project carried out in England on the historical knowledge and understanding of schoolchildren aged between 7 and 9 showed that they had derived about 85% of their knowledge of the past from sources other than school. We should not therefore underestimate the ideas, knowledge and experience acquired by schoolchildren outside the classroom.

It is helpful, in my view, to ponder the origins of our historical concepts and try to ascertain what can be proposed in each field in order to establish positive, effective criteria on the learning of history in a democratic, pluri-ethnic and multicultural society.

The teaching of history

History teaching should be aimed not so much at imparting specific contents as at enabling pupils to work out their own interpretations. It should not only focus on facts but also be aimed at developing certain skills. It should be vivid and, as 85% of the information acquired comes from out-of-school sources, these should be accorded much greater attention. Similarly, interaction between these sources should be fostered.

The amount of classroom time allocated to history teaching varies enormously from one country to another, but the aims of such teaching are largely identical, such as giving people a taste for history, making them active, responsible and critical citizens and showing them that historical truth cannot be reduced to one particular point of view. It is essential to find a way of talking to them about various historical events while comparing several sources of information and opinion, encouraging them to question their preconceived ideas and subjecting any event to a critical historical analysis. The role of politicians is to create conditions enabling history teachers to do their work more easily. There is an acute need for in-service training of teachers.

Improving school textbooks was the theme of the Council of Europe's first activity in the field of education, and the importance of history was emphasised by the European Cultural Convention as long ago as 1954. By this convention, each contracting party promises to "encourage the study by its own nationals of the languages, history and civilisation of the other contracting parties and grant facilities to those parties to promote such studies in its territory, and endeavour to promote the study of its [...] history and civilisation in the territory of the other contracting parties and grant facilities to the nationals of those parties to pursue such studies in its territory."

For some time it has been clear that teaching, especially history teaching, should continually reform its methods in order to be more effective. History is at the centre of the education system on account of its close links with the human sciences, which used to be called the "humanities" and are now called the "social sciences". History is, broadly speaking, central to culture in general, knowledge of the world, civic education, the organisation of societies and information about human beings and their virtues and defects. Lastly, history is the key element in education for children and young people, their knowledge and their ability to understand and criticise. A highly respected teacher, Joan Reglá, wrote an introduction to history which he entitled *Understanding the world*.

An education in history is therefore very important and requires continuous methodological and political thinking. If pupils are to be offered a perfectly sound, intelligible history in tune with the problems of our age – as would be desirable – it is important that syllabuses, learning methods and teaching staff should be routinely reassessed. This is a great challenge for public authorities, who need to ensure that the content of history syllabuses is as rigorous as possible and guarantees full freedom for historians. They must also make an effort to adjust teaching to present-day requirements and provide it with the latest audiovisual techniques.

The new information and communication tools (video, computers, CD-I, CD-Rom, and so on) offer a wide range of possibilities for facilitating the learning of history at school and elsewhere, provided that the intellectual quality is ensured. Educational methods should be differentiated, as they cannot be the same in primary education as in upper secondary education, where the content can be more sophisticated. As for universities, they can take advantage of an even more advanced technological potential. This learning should in any event be supplemented by other media, such as museums, television, cinema, visits to historic places and study of the arts.

As mentioned by Professor Prats at the Paris Colloquy, it is not a question for pupils of memorising historical facts but of learning through discovery. They should be given an opportunity to develop their understanding and critical sense by emphasising human behaviour in the past. The quality of education should take precedence over the quantity of information provided. In this way history can become a tool for dealing with the complexity of our age and planning the future. As Braudel stated, "history is a study of the origin of present-day problems".

Research

Teaching and research remain interdependent. The former could not evolve without the findings of the latter. However, historical errors result from interpretations by historians, researchers and teachers – who are often incidentally, one and the same person. Every year an enormous quantity of history books are published in all our countries. This may be good for the publishing trade, but the value and reliability of these short anecdotal histories or long wide-ranging theses is very varied. There is no planning of research or co-ordination between research, publishing and university teaching.

Public authorities should try to create conditions favourable to history research, provided that the research is independent of official policies.

Consideration could be given to encouraging a study of major topics that are currently controversial, such as foreign participation in the Spanish civil war, Stalinism, fascism, racism, minorities and national identities. Research should be carried out into concrete subjects capable of throwing light on our present.

Research (and the publication of its results) is the best remedy for manipulation and ignorance. It is the only means of restoring historical rigour.

Towards historical literacy

by David Lowenthal[1]

The perversions of history are not easily overcome. One reason is that they are pervasive. So engrained is our traditional view that history should be an impartial, objective, openly accessible record of the past – an ideal espoused by historians since Herodotus, Thucydides, and Lucian – that we either overlook or are aghast to learn that history is seldom so written, even by ardent devotees of its purity.

Well into the eighteenth century history was a *speculum vitae humanae*, an "impartial mirror" of men's actions and duties. The recording angel's detached neutrality was the Enlightenment vision. Aspiring to be "disengaged from all passions and prejudices", the Abbé Raynal claimed that future readers would find in his *Histoire philosophique et politique des deux Indes* (1781) no clue to his country, his profession or his religion. Diderot held detachment essential to understanding; only a "historian raised above all human concerns" could make sense of the protean past. Of course, no such historian existed, then or now.

In 1900 Lord Acton exhorted Britons to interpret European history with lofty impartiality; "our account of Waterloo must be one that satisfies French and English, Germans and Dutch alike". Acton's *Cambridge Modern History*, whatever its virtues, signally failed in this respect. Ethnocentrism and historical chauvinism are no less common today; and we are all constantly tempted to use history to inflate reputations, to deny past cruelties, to dispense comfort and to rationalise bias.

---

1. This speech was written for the colloquy "The learning of history in Europe" (Paris, 1994). David Lowenthal is a historian and geographer.

Rewriting the past to accommodate group pride is too human to be viewed as part of a conspiracy. Nor is it necessarily sinister to manipulate national history, as each of us always does with our personal life story. Indeed, it is all but unavoidable. The real issue historians face is how objective truth can be produced by deeply subjective people.

History as actually written is usually moral code as well as past record. In the words of Fustel de Coulanges, "the historian of the city told the citizen what he must believe and what he must adore" – or despise; the gallery of mythical royal rogues limned by the seventeenth-century Swedish historian Johannes Magnus called to readers' minds the evils of Gustavus Vasa. Chroniclers shaped accounts to please patrons, to praise compatriots, and to aggrandise their own repute. Early annalists unabashedly puffed sponsors; later historians promoted patriotism, which shapes history teaching to this day.

Histories stressing the innate superiority of ancestral forebears served nineteenth-century nationalism. "History is above all the science of national self-awareness", a Russian historian bluntly put it. Universal schooling aided this sacred function. A century ago 80% of French students of the *baccalauréat* held history's main purpose was to exalt patriotism; history teachers in 1919 saw making French citizens as their chief role. French history is still the touchstone of civilisation. Three-fourths of England's school history concerns British deeds and characters.

Profits and patriotism sway school histories to expunge the infamous, the awkward, even the debatable: one American publisher would omit not only "controversial" past notables like Roosevelt and Nixon, but any "living people who might possibly become infamous". The dubious future is consigned to oblivion along with the discreditable past. No historical event or figure must offend any minority's self-esteem.

Those who condemn patriotic or feel-good history are often its unwitting practitioners. Insisting that "disinterested intellectual inquiry" is the only valid approach, the historian Arthur Schlesinger Junior denounces those who exploit history as an instrument of social cohesion. But no sooner are these words out of his mouth than he claims that "above all, history can give us a sense of national identity".

Civic goals are not necessarily compatible with good scholarship. "Accurate history may teach us to get along together, but then again, it may not," writes a critic. Does our desire for an inclusive European vision ineluctably emerge from a cold, dispassionate examination of our chequered past? Is it forced on us by the overwhelming weight of evidence? No – it is projected into the past by our current desire to make it true.

Some historians reject *parti-pris* history. Myth and invention may be needed for people to say "We are different from and better than the others". Memories of past oppression persist as signs of allegiance; unless you share the myths that breed suspicion of others, you are a traitor to your own group. But those who promote this view are bad historians, holds Eric Hobsbawm. "History is not ancient memory or collective tradition." Historians should "stand aside from the passions of identity politics – even if they also feel them."

But many renowned historians openly promote myth for the sake of some higher truth. "Getting its history wrong is part of being a nation", Renan warned the French against excessive zeal for historical accuracy. English historians praise their precursors' muddled thinking as a national virtue. "We made our peace with the Middle Ages by misconstruing it. "False" history was one of our strengths," exulted Butterfield. Precisely because they did not know the Middle Ages, the historians of the time gave the seventeenth century just the type of anachronism that it required – mistaking the new English Constitution for a restoration of ancient liberties. Useful because mistaken, this version became a cornerstone of the national heritage. It buttresses self-esteem to this day. Unfazed by its exposure as a tissue of errors, the British revel in unreason. Opposing a 1993 bill in the House of Lords to allow daughters to inherit titles, the historian Trevor-Roper acclaimed male primogeniture for its traditional "irrationality".

Swiss heritage likewise favoured received myth over precise truth. Texts should be rectified only with great caution, warned an educator in 1872, for the Swiss saw history as "a school of patriotism". To destroy faith in traditions "that in their eyes symbolise liberty, independence and republican virtues" would corrode that patriotism. Besides, historical subtleties were "not the affair of the masses". William Tell's defiance of the Habsburg oppressor is a notorious fiction, but the tale is too pivotal to Swiss identity to be given up.

Irish celebratory chronicle is also held "a beneficial legacy, its wrongness notwithstanding". Past myths were punctured at the cost of their "positive dynamic thrust", warns the historian Brendan Bradshaw; to depopulate Irish history of heroes of national liberation would forfeit an immemorial treasure and "make the modern Irish aliens in their own land". When Ireland "has come of age", supposes revisionist Roy Foster, "history need no longer be a matter of guarding sacred mysteries," but until then the grand celebratory narrative is essential. "They all know it's not true", says Briege Duffaud's *Belfast Catholic* of the received mythos, "but that won't stop them believing it".

Fiction resists historical fact in order to perpetuate the legend. Daniel Boone's repeated disclaimers never dented the spurious antisocial legends spread of him. Parson Weem's fabrications of George Washington have been "shattered again and again", historians note, "but they live on in the popular mind, and nothing can extirpate them". Maori origin myths known to derive from European missionaries and traders are none the less accepted as ancestral because now embedded within Maori tradition. The "ancient" Breton folklore classic *Barzaz-Breiz*, though long surmised and now exposed as a nineteenth-century pastiche, is still accepted as the authentic voice of the Breton people because six generations have used it to express that voice. Breton identity "is not what history bequeathed them", writes Jean-Yves Guiomar, "but what romantic reconstruction or evolutionary progressivism has led them to build".

It is a sacrosanct Greek credo that underground schools kept Hellenic culture alive under Turkish oppressors, yet it is well known that Greek schooling in fact enjoyed widespread autonomy during Ottoman rule. When a 1960s schoolteacher was pilloried for questioning the legend, a prominent Greek explained that "even if the *krypha skholeia* was a myth, none the less it should still continue to be propagated, for such myths were an essential element in the national identity".

Commending error for history's sake is the theme of Joseph Roth's *Radetsky March*, whose Slovene protagonist is ennobled for rescuing the Emperor Franz Joseph at the battle of Solferino. Years later, in his son's first primer, he reads a grotesquely inflated version of the episode. "It's a pack of lies," he yells, throwing down the book. "It's for children," his wife replies. "Captain, you're taking it too seriously," says a friend; "all historical events are modified for consumption in schools. And quite right, too. Children need examples which they can understand, which impress them. They can learn later what actually occurred." The Minister for Culture and Education reiterates the point: "Without sacrificing veracity" school readers must provide "imaginative stimulus" to patriotism. The emperor himself rejects the literal truth. "It's a bit awkward," he admits, "but [...] neither of us shows up too badly in the story. Forget it."

Historians realise that history always attenuates truth. But this deficiency is little known and largely denied by the rest of us. Bereaved by the loss of the past, we take comfort in trusting it can be discerned without error or bias. But only by professional expertise: faithful retrieval is supposedly reserved to objective, dispassionate, infallible historians.

That historians are not such paragons most of them well know. Indeed, they repeatedly disclaim perfection. New-found evidence, revisionist criticism, stubborn bias, simple obsolescence remind historians they are inescapably fallible. But their disavowals fail to dispel popular faith that history, and history alone, can unearth and narrate the real Truth. Yet self-interest suffuses history like other enterprises. In theory, "historians are not allowed to use the past for their own ends," reflects a writer whose fictional historian (like most real ones) has just done so. How then, she asks, do historians differ from "politicians, house agents, antique dealers, autobiographers or any other category of person that does so most of the time?"

Perhaps historians bend the past to private ends more rarely and less blatantly. No doubt they are more conscious of doing so. Almost certainly, historians better recognise the gulf between precept and practice. More than house agents or antique dealers, they rate the truth of the past above its material benefits to themselves. But in choosing and conveying that "truth" they are bound to alter and update it according to their own lights. Historians do aim higher than they can reach. They know they cannot retrieve or recount the past in unbiased entirety or shorn of anachronism, yet they strive to do so as far as they can. Aware such effort is inherently imperfect, they none the less cleave to what seems honest and impartial.

Historical truth is praiseworthy. But public faith that historians can realise this goal taxes the task with delusive hopes. How can the public at large be encouraged to view history as neither a perfect record of the past nor a conspiracy to deprive them of their rightful heritage?

That children know too little history and get much of it wrong is a plaint re-echoed each generation. But the primary problem is not students' lack of canonical facts; it is that they do not know what history is in the first place. High marks depend on regurgitating historical facts and giving them the "correct" gloss; alternatives are only good or bad, right or wrong: honest differences are not an option. Asked to decide between two versions of an event, a student says, "It was cool to hear both sides of the story and choose who you think was telling the truth." "Both sides"! "Truth"! History becomes only a law court; every story has just two sides; whoever was wrong must have lied.

Three insights are integral to historical understanding: firstly, that history is never completely nor finally known; secondly, that its witnesses are never impartial; and thirdly, that we must avoid "presentist" anachronism as far as we can.

First, let us stress the contingency of history. At present, schools instil faith in historical truth. History is taught like mathematics – "as a finite subject with definite right or wrong answers". Most history texts are written as if their authors did not exist, as if they were simply instruments of a divine intelligence transcribing official truths – eighteenth-century recording angels. Students learn to accept these texts as authoritative vehicles whose sources are not to be questioned. Most of us learnt history as did Simone de Beauvoir, never dreaming there could be more than one view of past events. We should instead be trained to realise "there are no free-floating details – only details tied to witnesses".

To show that history and the way we interpret it is not carved in granite, that the past can never be totally reconstructed, that the study of history is always unfinished, one history museum stresses how provisional its findings are.

We're not saying, "This is the past. Believe it!" We're saying, "Given what we know, this is our best interpretation of the past. [Children should] learn that we're constantly finding out things that change our perception of the past. They'll learn that what we know about the past today is not what we'll know about the past in the future. They'll also learn that there are some things we can never find out."

This laudable lesson is too seldom taught or accepted.

Secondly, we should teach that history is inevitably biased because, written by fallible, partisan human beings, it demonstrates just how to assess and compare the voices of eye-witnesses, commentators, and authors. Historians who plead for awareness of bias seldom explain how to recognise it. The ability to see texts as slippery, cagey, protean, as instruments crafted for social ends, as reflections of manifold contexts and authors' concerns, is a skill unheard of in school and, indeed, much university history. To those lacking such insight, bias seems simply inexcusable and truth a clear-cut goal. This is why so many mistake historians' professed ideals for working realities.

Thirdly, awareness of anachronism. We may enjoy replacing fable and error with truth, but historians' main aim is not to debunk but to understand the past, to realise why people acted as they did. We must remember that the past is truly a foreign country, a congeries of mental worlds we have lost. Only thus can we avoid judging past actors as praiseworthy or perfidious, inconsistent or hypo-critical by today's standards, yet retain faith in history as a continuous nourishing tradition.

In the end, we can only partially affect how history is learned. In his classic *Everyman his own historian*, Carl Becker showed how most of us fashion patterns of the past, from things learned at home and in school, from knowledge gained in business and profession, from newspapers glanced at, from books [...] read or heard of, from remembered scraps of newsreels or educational films or *ex-cathedra* utterances of presidents and kings, from fifteen-minute discourses on the history of civilisation broadcast by Pepsodent.

From such heterogeneous sources *Everyman his own historian* chronicles more or less adequate impressions of the past.

The usual historical pastiche is as incoherent in 1990s Britain as in 1930s America. Neal Ascherson finds a melange of ill-remembered lessons, what father did in the war, television documentaries with half the instalments missed, bodice-ripper historical novels, fragments of local folklore, the general idea of what that Frenchman seems to be saying on the train, what we saw of Edinburgh Castle before the wee boy got sick, several jokes about Henry VIII and that oil painting of the king lying dead on the battlefield with his face all green.

Formal history is at once overlain, undermined, and fructified by other apprehensions of times gone by. To discern these connections is a goal well begun in France by Pierre Nora and his collaborators. Let it animate history throughout Europe.

SELECTION OF SYLLABUS CONTENT

by Joaquim Prats i Cuevas[1]

In recent years there have been numerous instances of governments changing curricula/syllabuses as well as the criteria for selecting curriculum/syllabus content, and there have also been many educationists working on curriculum/syllabus models. Traditionally there have been three approaches to this question of curriculum design, approaches which have found varying degrees of political favour or have matched developments in educational thinking. This paper briefly describes these approaches and the problems they have posed and continue to pose. It should be noted that this paper is not concerned with questions of historiography but rather with the criteria, or viewpoints, upon which history syllabuses have traditionally been based, both in primary and secondary education.

Traditional criteria in curriculum/syllabus design

Emphasis on national history

This is perhaps the most traditional approach, originating in a nineteenth century and early twentieth century outlook, and is still the commonest. Last century's triumphant middle classes saw history as an excellent means of shaping consciousness and underpinning the social and political structures of the state. (For that reason "state" is perhaps a more accurate word than "nation" in this context.) This tendency created an attitude to history, pervading all curricula and textbooks, that saw as the main object the handing down of a one-nation concept of a country's history. In other words,

---

1. This speech was written for the colloquy "The learning of history in Europe" (Paris, 1994). Joaquin Prats i Cuevas is professor of modern history at Lleida University.

history was regarded as serving the state. Nationalism has in fact been a frequent user and misuser of history. Early on, Topolsky was writing that "history and historical knowledge are the main ingredients of national consciousness and among the basic pre-requisites for the existence of any nation". This view is still to be found today.

In France in the early 1980s, for example, there was great debate when Michel Debré and the Committee for the Independence and Unity of France pointed out the risks to French people's education of approving a history syllabus which was not centrally concerned with the study of French national history. Ranged against them were the advocates of education as discovery, who took a relativist view and argued that history was an excellent body of knowledge for developing intellectual capability and bringing critical faculties to bear on social messages and phenomena. There have been similar debates in many other countries. In the United States at present there is debate about a Californian university's suggestion that history syllabuses should be changed so as to give a more universal picture, in particular by devoting significant attention to the history of oriental civilisations, thereby reducing the present western and patriotic emphasis.

This phenomenon has been taken to dangerous extremes in pre-war periods, especially by totalitarian regimes. The previous regime in Spain was one example. While the patriotic slant was to be found in syllabuses at the beginning of the century, the tendency became very marked during the Franco dictatorship, a regime that justified itself as the protector of Spain's distinctiveness from the "evil" of liberal or social ideas originating elsewhere, more particu-larly in Europe. The glories of imperial Spain and Spanish wars against foreign powers, such as the war of independence against revolutionary France, were thus reaffirmed. "Unity of destiny in the universal" was a slogan of the dictatorial system. Distortions of such an exaggerated kind have currently given way to a weakening of this approach in curricula, perhaps by way of reaction, and the risk we now run is that of a glorification of regional or local history, with the attendant danger of promoting a new form of "chauvinism" coupled with the isolationist attitudes resulting from overestimating the importance of one's own heritage.

History as a means of transforming the present versus "fragmented history"

In this approach the history of mankind is regarded as a process of continuous progress. The view of history as a central element in the education of the progressively-minded future citizen has been highly successful of late, or at least this has been the case in countries such as Spain. The saying of the Spanish historian, Josep Fontana, that "history is a weapon in today's struggles and a tool for building the future" perfectly sums up the role which history teaching should play according to this approach. It is an approach which involves deciding the methods and, indeed, the content of history teaching with the goal of making it as scientific an instrument as possible for the rigorous analysis and potential transformation of society.

Here, subject content is not primarily geared to the study of a particular national or regional history but focuses rather on the structure of the particular social model, the different types of society and their implications for the various social groups and classes. National history can provide a good testing ground, but the object is not to promote awareness of belonging to a distinctive national community but instead to teach how society functions and about the forces for changing it.

As a result of the crisis which history as an academic discipline seems to be going through, that approach is very much in decline. When Francis Fukuyama proclaims the end of history, the permanence and immutability of the system is deified, and, whether on a conscious or unconscious level, this view has in fact met with a fairly sympathetic reception. If Fukuyama is right, history ceases to have educational value as an awareness-shaper for helping to bring about social change. There seem to be more and more teachers who believe that the syllabus should cover only narrow aspects of historical knowledge. In other words, François Dosse would appear to be right when he describes the present trend as being towards a fragmentation of historical knowledge and away from a well-rounded approach to history. Dosse sees history as the target for takeover bids by the social sciences and believes that history could cease to be a subject in its own right, turning into a miscellany of unrelated ingredients or a purely accessory body of knowledge. The signs are here of the emergence of a new, positivist, event-centred school of history concerned with the factual and the anecdotal and which does not think in terms of, or recognise, any overall social dynamic. This is the diametrical opposite of the broad-brush, social-transformation brand of history which was so popular in the 1960s and 1970s. Pierre Vilar's dictum that any modern approach to history is necessarily a "macro" approach seems to have gone out of fashion.

History as a means to personal development and the propagation of social attitudes and ideas

History is undoubtedly the subject area most inclined to ideology. It also lends itself to the treatment of ideas, attitudes and values. On occasions it has been used to fly the flag for antithetical political stances (such as racism-antiracism, belligerence-passivism, authoritarianism-liberalism). Some recent theorists, such as Rotheiv, see the history syllabus as commemorating not only oppression, injustice and suffering, but equally the endeavours to put an end to them. History so conceived, adopting neither a materialist nor an out-and-out idealist approach, becomes an excellent means of cultivating particular ethical and social values.

There is also a school of thought that sees history solely as a means to cognitive or personality development. Even though this is a minority tendency, represented by educational psychologists and laymen rather than historians, there is a degree of receptiveness to it in some areas of primary teaching. Which is not to deny that such objectives are inherent in any intellectual activity and need drawing attention to in any discussion of education. But they cannot be made into the main criteria of syllabus design without discarding the central reference to historical knowledge, without which it ceases to be history that is being taught.

As already mentioned, none of these three brands of history is ever practised quite as described. History teaching tends to be much more eclectic and to combine the various emphases; development of communal identity with other much more academic considerations, inculcation of values and attitudes with the teaching of intellectual skills and procedures. What, then, are the items of historical knowledge that need incorporating into the learning process?

With what type of historical knowledge should the learning process be concerned?

A quite separate development is that in recent decades some history teachers and history-teaching theorists have put forward new criteria for drawing up history syllabuses, increasingly distancing themselves from the concerns of practising historians of the day. One of the reasons for this, no doubt, is the difficulty of teaching history in primary and secondary school. Our view is that the syllabus needs to combine the teaching of subject-related skills with the teaching of European history. It has to be stressed that the emphasis is on providing pupils with genuine learning opportunities and that no particular regard is had for the requirements of the academic historian. Selection of syllabus content is based on two considerations: firstly, the impossibility, in primary and secondary school, of teaching the whole of history and secondly, the need to develop some knowledge and awareness of things "historical". The concern must be to develop basic general skills relevant to the understanding of history, and for that purpose there are any number of historical topics – local, regional, national or universal – that can be used. Without seeking to be exhaustive, we can identify various types of syllabus content that can be presented differently, in terms both of events covered and periods of history selected. A number of examples follow.

Firstly, we have topics providing material for the study of chronology and historical timescale. The focus here is on one of the distinctive ingredients of history: time and rates of change. Pupils are brought to realise the conventional nature of units of time, are introduced to such complex questions as time/causality in history, develop an awareness of continuity through time, and acquire an understanding of different rates of historical development.

Secondly, there is the study of events, people and factors that have played a key role in history. The focus is on past occurrences. In recent years there has been some retreat from this approach, which tended to be confused with the kings-and-battles approach to history. However, this type of syllabus content needs reinstating and using in the context of a broader, more explanatory approach. There is room here for work on areas of local history and major past events, providing it is geared to developing an overarching conceptual model and learning to apply a broad frame of reference.

Thirdly, we have topics related to the ideas of change and continuity. Taking issue with more structuralist tendencies which advocate a compartmentalised treatment of the past, we recommend highlighting the concepts of continuity and change. There are four main aspects of these questions.

Firstly, change takes time, and is sometimes very fast (see, for example, the present pace of change) and sometimes slow (for example changes in the rural way of life in the fourteenth and fifteenth centuries).

Secondly, in any given historical period the rate of change varies from one society to another, and the pupil therefore has to learn to make a distinction between the continuum of historical time and the processes and events which occur within it;

Thirdly, change is not a continuous process and has not always been for the better nor been progressive. Pupils readily confuse change and progress, and when working with a class of adolescents in the throes of maturing into adults, the teacher has to make it very clear that scales of value vary from one society to another. But attention must be paid to periods of rapid change during which events gathered pace and there was a social, political or cultural leap forward.

Lastly, there is investigation of the causes of past events. Concepts of historical causality are complex and historians do not always agree about them. For that reason it is advisable to choose syllabus items that bring out the difficulty and complexity of identifying the causes of particular events. In a democratic society it is educationally valuable to combat dogmatism and mechanistic explanations, and the study of history brings out the complexity of human affairs better than any other subject. Getting pupils to see history as a process of continuous change in which our present way of life has evolved, leads to teaching them to ask questions about the causes of change as well as about factors which have prevented or delayed it. And to understand the causes of a given historical occurrence, they have to learn to consider what reasons people or social groups had for acting as they did.

The learning process

A syllabus of the kind described is unworkable where the learning process involves total pupil passivity and the pupil role is confined to receiving chunks of evaluated, processed and pre-digested knowledge. The teaching approach we suggest – without dismissing the possibility of others equally effective – is one of discovery learning, involving pupils in the use of information sources and making it possible for pupils to assemble their own knowledge of historical facts and concepts with the teacher's help and guidance. In accordance with this approach, we regard the pupil as the main actor in the education process and not as a mere receiver of instruction. The teacher's role mainly consists of steering, co-ordinating and initiating the learning process.

Another basic principle is the application of methodological categories, advancing from the concrete to the abstract. In this way learning will be slow but will progress from a solid base and on a rising curve. Use and thorough mastery of some of the historian's techniques, such as observing, describing, analysing, relating, hypothesising, extrapolating, evaluating and generalising, will equip the pupils to handle historical facts and events properly.

Learning can be in two stages:

– In the first, the pupil acquires the knowledge and skills for using the historian's basic tools. The syllabus covers the question of historical sources and the different types of historical source and the pupil learns the conventions of chronology, learns how to extract information from sources, and develops the general skills of analysis, assessment and comparison necessary for an understanding of historical fact.

– Once the content of the first stage has been adequately assimilated, pupils are able to move on to the second stage and tackle actual items of history: explore a particular event in depth, study a society at a given moment, study historical processes, and investigate the historical roots of contemporary issues. The object is to provide a kind of historiographical simulation exercise that gives pupils an insight into the nature of historical knowledge, without dispensing it, however, from school textbooks or teacher's explanations. This is also the point at which to administer a modicum of theory so as to introduce pupils to the problems of interpretation. This type of simulation exercise can be used from a very early stage. Its effectiveness depends on the basic subject matter, which the pupils have to find interesting, as well as on the clarity of the aims and methods, and on the information sources, which must be limited in number. It is for the teacher to direct the work and to supply narrative links and overall sense to what is being learned.

This approach to the teaching of history is not an easy one for the teacher to use at secondary level, and is even less so at primary level. However, if we set out to aid pupils' intellectual development and, through the study of history, equip them to analyse the present instead of emphasising rote learning of historical fact or using history as an ideological instrument, there is no doubt that this approach will give pupils a better grasp of historical concepts and promote more dynamic and more meaningful learning. Education is a basic factor in the harmonious development of adolescents, and we believe that it is important not just to know history but also to acquire civic attitudes, that is, democratic, tolerant and responsible attitudes.

But going through the facts of history is no way to instil those attitudes. What is needed is a grasp of how historical knowledge is constructed. This will provide a key to understanding history and analysing the present, and will facilitate the development of pupils' critical faculties, which are vital to an education based upon freedom.

THE CATHOLIC CHURCH AND THE TEACHING OF HISTORY

by Roland Minnerath[1]

Christians believe that God intervenes in history, that He revealed himself and became incarnate in it, and that He is leading it towards fulfilment. He thus dignifies human history in a special way. A distinction needs to be made here between:

– *salvation history*: God's interventions in history (creation, covenant, prophets, incarnation, redemption, foundation of the Church, eschatology). This involves a theological approach to history, which is interested more in the deeper meaning than in the details of what happened;

– *empirical history* (which historians study with the appropriate methods): this attempts to reconstruct the events and the meaning which protagonists gave them with maximum objectivity.

All teachers of history interpret events as well as recount them. Their interpretation of history is influenced by subjective elements – their cultural backgrounds, aims and own viewpoints. The meaning of history is never immanent in history itself, but is the product of a broader interpretation of events by the observer. Hence the need to look out for prejudices and ideologies which project artificial and inadequate interpretations onto the past.

The Church's approach to the teaching of history operates on several levels: it focuses on the main themes of salvation history (the theology of history); at the same time, it applies critical methods to the study of sources, drawing on archaeology, linguistics and historical methods. Specifically, it relates biblical history to the literary form of the texts concerned (the Prophets, the Books of

---

1. This speech was written for the colloquy "The learning of history in Europe" (Paris, 1994). Roland Minnerath is professor of ecclesiastical history at Strasbourg University and Advisor to the Secretariat of State of the Holy See.

Wisdom, the Gospels, the Acts, the Epistles, and so on) and puts them in the historical context known from other sources.

The Church's own history is also part of the history it teaches. In certain periods, "Church history" and "history" more or less co-incide. Until around 1945, Church histories were written either from national or narrowly denominational standpoints, with all the prejudices inherent in these approaches. In fact, the very concept of catholicity is inclusive, rather than exclusive, and the trans-national, transcultural nature of Church history offers a possible pattern for the writing of European or world history in a way that transcends partial interpretations.

The Catholic Church's teaching of history is not only religious in the strict sense of the term. In its social teaching, the Church also bases Christian ethics on its reading of economic, social, cultural, con-tinental and, indeed, world history.

In Christianity, it is the Word of God, handed down by tradition – and not historically observable empirical behaviour – which sets the standards. The study of history can help us to develop a critical attitude towards events we have lived through ourselves, and detach ourselves from them when necessary.

In the view of history transmitted by the Church, God stands at the beginning and the end of human history. God is the criterion which gives us a proper perspective on the things which we are tempted to regard as absolutes, and which generate exclusion and conflict – power, nations, parties, money, and so on.

If God is the judge of history, then God also suggests the values which allow us to shape it in a manner worthy of humankind. The failures of the past must not have the last word. Hope is also part of the Christian view of history.

TOWARDS A BASIC CONCEPT OF HISTORICAL LITERACY

by Maitland Stobart[1]

Introduction

History and history teaching have always occupied a special place in the Council of Europe's work on education because of their importance in establishing mutual understanding and confidence between the peoples of Europe. The improvement of history textbooks was the subject of the Council's first activity on education, and the importance of history is stressed in the European Cultural Convention of 1954.

This convention sets the framework for the Council of Europe's work on education, culture, heritage, sport and youth. All contracting parties undertake to encourage the study, by their nationals, of the history of the other contracting parties. They also agree to promote the study of their own history in the territory of the other dontracting parties and to grant facilities to the nationals of those parties to pursue such studies in their territory.[2]

The Council of Europe's work on history has been carried out in two stages. The first was an attempt, mainly in the 1950s, to encourage the highest standards of honesty and fairness in history textbooks, and to eradicate bias and prejudice. In the second stage, the Council studied the place of history in secondary schools and drew up recommendations on how to make history a stimulating and relevant part of a young person's education.

---

1. This speech was written for the colloquy "The learning of history in Europe" (Paris, 1994). Maitland Stobart is Deputy Director for Education, Culture and Sport at the Council of Europe.

2. As of 1997, forty-four states have acceded to the convention: The Council of Europe's forty member states and Belarus, the Holy See, Monaco and Bosnia and Herzegovina.

In the past seven years, there has been a significant revival of interest in history teaching in Europe, and the Council of Europe has started a new series of activities on the subject.

Can we, to a certain extent, clarify the idea of a basic concept of historical literacy? Strictly speaking, of course, "literacy" is "the ability to read and write", and some purists strongly object to the use of the term in other contexts. Nevertheless, it can be used as a convenient label or shorthand term to cover the mastery of a body of content, skills and attitudes. Thus, people often speak of "political literacy", "computer literacy", "cultural literacy" and even "moral literacy". This is the way in which I will use the term in my presentation, and I will relate the Council of Europe's thinking on history to the three key components: content, skills and attitudes. All three are important, and "historical literacy" is not synonymous with the rote learning of a set of facts.

The Council of Europe is, of course, aware that schools are not the only source of information, education and opinion and that other influential sources are: the family, the peer-group, the local and national community, the mass media, and tourism. We should, therefore, not under-estimate the ideas, knowledge and experience that pupils bring with them to the classroom.

Schools are important because they are the official agents of socialisation. They provide young people with the skills and attitudes to use information in a rigorous and responsible way; help them to understand the complexity of political, social and economic issues and to appreciate cultural diversity; and dispel stereotypes avoiding a simplistic "headline mentality".

The value and scope of history

The Council of Europe's experts recommend that all pupils should study history at every level of their education because history has a value that cannot be provided by other subjects in the school curriculum. "History", they argue, "is a unique discipline, concerned with a special kind of training of the mind and imagination and with the imparting of an accurate body of knowledge which ensures that pupils understand other points of view".

History can help pupils to grasp the relationship of events in time so that they can appreciate such essential concepts as cause and effect, change and development.

With regard to the scope of history, the Council's experts propose that it should be the learning and teaching of a synthesis dealing not only with political, diplomatic and military history, but with all aspects – spiritual, social, economic, cultural, scientific and technological – of the societies of the past.

The learning and teaching of history in schools should be an active process, and it should stimulate individual research, reflection and expression by pupils. They should be given experience in the critical evaluation of different kinds of evidence, and they should be encouraged to adopt critical attitudes towards information, including that imparted by the mass media. For example, in history, pupils should learn to "read" films and television programmes as critically as they should read newspapers.

Content

With regard to content, the Council of Europe's experts argue that there is no specific body of historical knowledge that every pupil ought to learn. Furthermore, all of our meetings have shown that there is a problem of finding a happy balance between local, national, European and world history in history curricula.

Local history lends itself to active methods and can help to train pupils in historical method and see larger problems in microcosm. For its part, national history should not be isolated from its

European and world contexts, and pupils should be encouraged to see the European importance of, and the European influences on, events of national history.

In the present volatile situation in Europe, there is a new sensitivity about national and ethnic identity. Identity is a complex concept which covers: language; religion; and a shared memory and a sense of history, sometimes even of historical grievance and injustice. It is rich in symbols: heroes; battles lost and won; songs; poetry; paintings and memorials. Sometimes identity asserts itself in a destructive and violent way at the expense of the identity of others: migrants, immigrants, minorities, and peoples of other nationalities, religions and races. History should not encourage narrow chauvinistic, intolerant attitudes or lead to feelings of ethnic, national or racial superiority.

National history is not synonymous with nationalistic history, and there is an urgent need to explore new balanced approaches to the learning and teaching of national history.

We sometimes hear calls for a single European history syllabus or a single European history textbook for use in all our schools. Is this feasible in an area stretching from North Cape to Cyprus and Malta and from Reykjavik to Berlin, Warsaw and Vladivostok? Is it even desirable? Our experts have been adamant that there can be no question of trying to impose a uniform version of European history in schools throughout our continent.

Certain elements are, naturally, common to the history of part, or all, of Europe. Such topics as the great migrations, feudalism, the Renaissance, the religious reform movements, European expansion overseas, the Enlightenment, the Industrial Revolution, and communism and fascism lend themselves, therefore, to a European perspective.

In October 1993, the Vienna Summit of heads of state and government of the Council of Europe's member states stressed the urgent need to strengthen "programmes aimed at eliminating prejudice in the teaching of history by emphasising positive mutual influences between countries, religions and ideas in the historical development of Europe". As a follow-up to this recommendation, we are now carrying out a project to identify innovatory approaches to teaching the history of Europe in the spirit of the Vienna Declaration. Its results included a study on the European content of the school history curriculum and a practical handbook for teachers, *History teaching and the promotion of democratic values and tolerance*.

Sixteen states in central and eastern Europe now participate in the Council of Europe's education programme, and politicians, educators and young people in our new partner countries are often dismayed by the ignorance, in the older member states, of their history and culture. They argue that the Council of Europe has a duty to respond to this situation, for example by publishing, for history teachers in other parts of the continent, a series of booklets or teaching packs on the history of our new partner countries.

Whenever possible, national and European horizons should be widened to a world perspective, and other civilisations should be studied from the standpoint of their own original nature and not just in the context of European expansion and occupation. For its part, the Parliamentary Assembly has recommended that all of us should be aware of the distinctive contributions of Jewish culture and Islamic civilisation to the historical development of Europe.

The Council of Europe's experts are also convinced that all pupils should learn modern and contemporary history. This opinion is shared by the Parliamentary Assembly which has called for "the adequate teaching of modern history so that young people will be better prepared to promote democracy". Between 1997 and 1999, the Council of Europe will carry out an ambitious new project on learning and teaching about the history of Europe in the twentieth century in secondary schools. Its aim is to interest young people in the recent history of our continent and understand the forces, individuals, movements and events which have shaped Europe in the twentieth century.

Skills and attitudes

Among the skills associated with the learning of history, the Council of Europe's experts attach special importance to: the ability to locate, handle and analyse different forms of information and evidence; the ability to frame relevant questions and arrive at responsible and balanced conclusions; the ability to express oneself clearly, both orally and in writing; the ability to see other points of view and to recognise and accept differences; the ability to detect error, bias and prejudice.

The learning and teaching of history should also lead to the development of several important attitudes, in particular curiosity, open-mindedness, tolerance, empathy and civil courage. The learning of history should stimulate the imagination and provide both pleasure and enjoyment.

School links and exchanges, in particular, can help to develop understanding and friendship between young people from different linguistic, cultural, ethnic and religious traditions both within and between countries. In its new work on history, the Council of Europe is examining how the learning of history outside the classroom – through school links and exchanges, visits to museums, and field trips – can further mutual understanding and confidence in Europe.

Questions for reflection

In themselves, the Council of Europe's recommendations do not constitute a ready-made, common "basic concept of historical literacy". On the other hand, they do indicate many of the questions and elements which have to be faced in the daunting task of defining this challenging concept.

Our curricula, textbooks and the practices should conform to the following criteria:

They should:

– respect historical truth;

– uphold democratic institutions;

– promote human rights, tolerance, understanding and multi-perspectivity;

– develop critical thinking and the ability to recognise bias, prejudice and stereotypes;

– encourage such attitudes as open-mindedness, acceptance of diversity, empathy and civil courage.

Learning outside the educational system

The media

The media are a mass phenomenon capable of informing – or misinforming – hundreds of thousands of readers, listeners or viewers. History is both a beneficiary and a victim of this phenomenon. The media fulfil two functions: they disseminate information and analyses concerning the historical past and, at the same time, they produce documents on current events that will be the history of tomorrow.

The traditional means of disseminating historical knowledge – books, lectures, studies – reached only a limited section of society. Nowadays, thanks to written publications and audiovisual broadcasts, the average citizen has easier access to history. He or she also finds references to the past and historical analyses in the utterances of politicians.

Because of the immense power of images, television is undoubtedly the most effective communication medium for reaching the maximum number of people. It is therefore the ideal instrument for disseminating and teaching all kinds of knowledge, especially history, provided that it treats knowledge in a respectful manner.

For television, history has become a useful theme as it interests the general public. Some channels have scheduled historical series at peak viewing times on account of their success. A channel entirely devoted to history has even been considered.

However, the media are not always rigorous and are liable to trivialise historical facts and manipulate opinion. For technical, budgetary and audience-rating reasons, they cannot present the pros and cons that are essential to any historical analysis. The message is therefore curtailed. Some ethical rules should be observed by programme-makers, who should also secure the assistance of a historian.

A code of ethics might provide a yardstick for the treatment of history by the media.

Art and museums

Art is history, and museums are the repositories of history. Art, even in its contemporary form, translates the aesthetic and social thoughts and concerns of an age. Art is representative of its period, and in order to understand and interpret it, we need a knowledge of history, which, in turn, is enhanced through artistic experience.

Museums are an important adjunct to education in the same way as a visit to a castle. Fresh impetus has been given to artistic exhibitions, which are now more educational and historical. Interpretation of works is becoming more subtle and sensitive as a result.

If they are to be essential adjuncts to education, museums must, in order to be understandable, set off their collections to the best advantage by providing interpretations of them. The number of history museums should be increased at all levels – national, regional and local – on the pattern of the German "House of History" in Bonn.[1] Professional historians can help to enhance these museums, which are pages of history, and transform them into documentary evidence of the past.

---

1. See Hermann Schäfer's contribution p. 79.

Theatre and cinema

These two artistic disciplines are closely linked to history as they are wonderful instruments of historical dissemination. Although fictional, they sometimes give very accurate insights into history (French Revolution, fall of the Roman Empire, second world war, and so on) and invariably contain an explicit or implicit message.

When its historical analysis is accurate, even a fiction devoid of substance may provide us with knowledge of another age or an earlier way of life. And this can provide us with a better understanding than a serious history book by a well-known historian.

But we should be aware of confusing history-cinema (such as *A Man for All Seasons or Schindler's List*) with entertainment-cinema (such as *Cleopatra* or *Braveheart*). Their messages are very different for, while the former gives us a good insight into history, the latter is sadly lacking in historical rigour.

Literature

Literature, the whole of literature, is impregnated with history, and the historical element is very often present even in poetry : Bertold Brecht, Victor Hugo, Federico García Lorca and many others, not forgetting the epic poems.

Similarly, history belongs to literature. The historical approach is commonly introduced into novels, essays or other narrations. History is also a literary genre : history books, memoirs, biographies, travel books, chronicles, diaries, specialised review articles, encyclopaedias, and so on. Lastly, written history is also literature.

Some literary works have a very rich historical content. *The Name of the Rose, The Grapes of Wrath* and *Don Quixote* have provided us with more historical information and knowledge than many history books. The reconstruction of a historical period with full creative freedom sometimes offers a clearer overall picture than a doctoral thesis.

At the same time, the compulsory reading of such authors as Leon Tolstoy, Marguerite Yourcenar or Robert Graves serves to complement the educational process thanks to the historical approach underlying their novels. In the case of fiction, it is impossible to demand rigour and truth. But it is for teachers to restore the accuracy of the historical message in order to avoid any possible deviation.

The entourage: family, friends, community

Parents' opinions and whatever is recounted in the family setting are the earliest influences to which a child is subjected. Each family inherits an ancestral memory and expresses its views on the past and on politics and history. It provides a wealth of information about places, people and historical events, and prompts us to read this or that book. This instils in children certain tastes, fashions and ideologies that will shape their idea of history.

A child will acquire a wider view of history from journeys and meetings with different people.

On the other hand, history learning is nowadays a very complex process of accumulating information and absorbing interpretations, discourses and reconstructions, and it is constantly renewed as each day brings new historical references.

THE TELE-VISION OF HISTORY

by Klaus Wenger[1]

Television: source and product of history

History and the transmission of history are really all about memory and, more specifically, images. The collective memory is made up of images, be they complementary or contradictory, true or false, authentic or modified, or even doctored. The audiovisual media, and above all, television, rank among this century's largest producers of images.

The mass media and audiovisual technology have permeated all spheres of public and private life, and it is increasingly television which decides on the images which go to make up memory. Already it has very largely replaced schools, archives and books as vehicles of history. Everywhere, the spoken and written word are giving way to the image as the primary component of history.

This dominant position in the presentation of history ought to be matched by a greater sense of responsibility on the part of the producers of these images, notably journalists and programme makers.

Television is no longer a mere bystander, a relatively faithful or credible witness of current events: it is becoming one of the main vectors of the "writing" of contemporary history (the pictures of the signing of the Israeli-Arab peace agreement are an example).

---

1. This speech was written for the colloquy "The learning of history in Europe" (Paris, 1994). Klaus Wengeris is the head of the documentary unit of Arte, a Franco-German cultural television channel based in Strasbourg.

At the same time, television is itself a product of history; its visual language, its thematic and creative resources reflect a culture, an ideology and hence a historical situation.

Television's workings, status, purpose and objectives, as well as its influence, depend on the prevailing political and historical climate. Take for example the differences between the French and German audiovisual systems which are due to the role of the media during the second world war.

The audiovisual media, agents of history

A truism: the mass media contribute to the collective memory as much by their images as by what they do not show or tell.

Over the course of the twentieth century, the written word has gradually been replaced first by the spoken word and later by images. Remember the power of the radio between the 1920s and 1950s, its mobilising role in propaganda broadcasts under the nazi regime (*Der Führer spricht*) and the decisive role of radio in organising resistance activities in countries under *Wehrmacht* occupation, not to mention the panic triggered by Orson Welles' "martian attack" broadcast in the United States.

With radio, the audiovisual media also emerged as a cross-border historical protagonist, as in, for example, the appeals carried on Hungarian radio in 1956.

Technical progress, especially satellite broadcasting, means that pictures, and hence their impact on individuals or social groups, are no longer confined to a national or geopolitical area. At the same time it leads to the multiplication and globalisation of sources of information and pictures. The days when the mass media served to forge a national identity are over; there is no longer a single "voice of France" but a France reverberating to a profusion of voices.

Consequently, television can no longer serve as the rallying force behind a clear-cut view of history as was the case between the 1960s and the 1980s.

Let us not forget that, during that period, television, more than any other media, helped impose a specific view of the history of nations, particularly by marking out taboo areas or by tackling them – hence French television's silence on Vichy as opposed to efforts in the Federal Republic of Germany to come to terms with the National Socialist past.

The control of images and hence of the historical imagination is thus out of the sole hands of the political authorities. The state loses its monopoly over a tool which is vital for imposing and propagating its view of history. But, does this spell the end of official histories?

Image manipulation

There is less and less political or ideological manipulation of images at national or state level. It is therefore increasingly difficult to control or impose a consistent and calculated – political, religious, ideological – vision of history. The job of recounting and interpreting history thus gradually slips from the grasp of its traditional agents: historians, writers, politicians and so on.

Technical progress in broadcasting, particularly satellite, has allowed television to play a major role in departitioning Europe. The televised chronicle of the downfall of the communist empire is perhaps the finest example of television's role as an agent of history. These milestones illustrate the importance of television as an instrument and ingredient of intercultural dialogue in Europe.

At the same time, we witnessed television's worst excesses. The "death camps" in Romania, the staging of Ceaucescu's trial and the discovery of the video archives of central Europe highlight the danger of manipulative television. Other "productions" – the Gulf war or the live relay of the American military's intervention in Somalia or Haiti – show us the dangers of a medium imposing its law on political and socio-cultural forces: history is transformed into a global village reality show.

Let us also be on our guard against technological progress in fabricating images; digital images and the computer make it possible to constantly manipulate what is being broadcast. Computer and digital editing blur the concepts of original and copy, of authenticity and reconstitution. The image is no longer the reflection of a tangible reality, since that "reality" can be created by virtual images.

The audiovisual media's penetration of all facets of our everyday lives – video conferencing, video surveillance – generates a proliferation of images and sounds, which will become sources for historical research by future generations. How are we going to store this flood of material? How should the material be processed and interpreted? How can historians be trained to master these new sources?

The image will always serve to fuel our imaginations and therefore our visions of history. But its nature is changing: it is no longer a source which can be checked, if only against other testimonies; it is no longer the object of our reading or writing of history. The new technology of the image is changing the dominant position of our imagination and in so doing is transforming our relationship with history. History is again becoming what it always has been: a virtual approach to the past.

A MUSEUM DIRECTOR'S POINT OF VIEW

by Hermann Schäfer[1]

I hope I'm not going to scare you off at the outset with this introductory talk dealing with the role of history – given by somebody who is a history teacher and museum director into the bargain. This will probably depend on your recollection of history lessons and your teachers at that time. Yes, teachers, who according to a book written in 1985, are "hinderers and destroyers" in just about everything. This is certainly no sociological analysis, but a sarcastic exaggeration by the Austrian playwright Thomas Bernhard. I am quoting from his book *Old Masters* and he doesn't mean it all that seriously – sarcastic as he almost always is – because his book is subtitled "a comedy" : "Teachers have always been, on the whole, hinderers of life and existence; instead of teaching young people about life, explaining life to them, making it an inexhaustible treasure trove of their own nature, they stifle it, do everything to kill it off for them. The majority of our teachers are poor creatures, whose object in life appears to be to barricade life off from young people and finally make it something infinitely depressing. It is in fact only touchy and perverse petty minded people from the lower middle class who flock into teaching."

Did you have history teachers like that? The accusations are by no means new: as early as a hundred years ago, the Italian historian Benedetto Croze reproached German historians for having too little imagination and for being too pedantic and ponderous. He called instead for more lively and more accessible presentations.

Or did you prefer to go to a museum? How lively do you think German museums are? Already a hundred years ago German

---

1. This speech was written for the colloquy "The learning of history in Europe" (Paris, 1994). Hermann Schäfer is Director of the House of History Museum, in Bonn, Federal Republic of Germany.

curators complained that their visitors looked for texts everywhere and even to some extent seemed to want to "read with their ears". There is still something in this reproach today. Allow me to quote Thomas Bernhard again, this time making a very effective literarily comparison of the different European nations with regard to their behaviour in museums: "The Italians with their innate understanding of art always appear as if they were in the know since birth. The French go through the museum in a somewhat bored fashion, while the English act as if they know and understand everything. The Russians are full of wonder. The Poles look down on everything."

The Germans come off worst: "The Germans spend all their time in the art museum looking in the catalogue as they go through the rooms, and scarcely glance at the originals hanging on the walls. As they advance through the museum they go ever deeper into the catalogue until they reach the last page and find themselves outside again."

Last year our German museums received a total of one hundred million visitors, and not all of them behaved as we have just heard. On the whole this is satisfying, but these people make up only 30% of the population. My museum is therefore turning not so much to "museum freaks" as described by Thomas Bernhard, but rather towards ordinary people.

The school and the museum are two very different institutions, which therefore influence social reality in very different ways. From the school we expect a certain "basic equipment" for life, from the museum – especially the historical museum – an occasion for information and reflection.

Some years ago, Hermann Lübbe drew attention to the relationship between the accelerated progress of civilisation, the growing uncertainty among people and an increasing tendency to create museums. In other words, the faster our present life changes, the greater our desire to preserve the relics of our past life in museums and display them as points of reference for our thinking. Museums raise historical consciousness. They provide a retrospective of human culture, and thus establish lines of tradition and stimulate memory, which contributes in turn to the formation of a historic identity and self-reassurance. Seen in this way, the museum and its contents appear anything but fossilised and dusty, but are entirely constitutive of current thought and action. For only through confrontation with our history are we able to understand our present and shape our future in a responsible fashion. Thus the concept of "history" is a variable which can be partly replaced by life experience, personality, self-awareness or origin, and overlaps with these concepts.

Developments in Germany have confirmed this trend towards museum creation in a completely new and unexpected way. The West Germans were in the front seats when the iron curtain came down and – as the historian Theodor Mommsen said, "world history took a turn". A state does not collapse every day, and it is not only collectors and souvenir hunters who seize the opportunity to gather up the vestiges of a state, its civilisation and culture, but also museums. The placards and banners from the big demonstration of 4 November 1989 on Berlin's Alexanderplatz were already being exhibited five months later in Berlin and Bonn. One of my favourite banners from this exhibition reads "No future without a past".

This slogan obviously also applies to museums themselves. While they may, in the past, have been places of learning or temples to the muses, in the future they will have to be understood much more as places of entertainment. The museum is one of the media. The basic advantage of this particular medium, and certainly a reason for its popularity, is that it is not dependent on a specific target group. Exhibitions, even poor ones, do not speak the language of experts, but are organised so that the visitors themselves can find words and concepts for what they see, and put their thoughts about the objects exhibited in their own terms.

"Historical awareness is a complex interplay between memory of the past, interpretation of the present and expectation of the future" (Jeismann). The social significance of historical memory is thus by no means easy to define. Whether reflection on a common or partially separate history is capable of strengthening an identity – a feeling of community and mutual awareness leading to a consensus and an orientation (something required for the legitimacy of societies) – is today very much disputed. There is therefore no museological dogmatism to regulate or functionalise the use of the museum – and this is a good thing. The range of topics of historical museums is just as inexhaustible as are the historical perspectives and issues themselves. And the creativity of those designing exhibitions has long since evolved from the dry presentation of documents to the representation and symbolisation of history, positively extending the scope for both the conceptual and the instructional/didactic aspects.

A question constantly asked of the historical museum is: can history – and hence an understanding of the present – be taught in the museum?

A museum is not a school. It is not possible to mug up for an examination here. It is not a matter of teaching in the traditional sense of classes or lectures. The museum is more concerned with providing the experience of communication between the generations.

So far as the expectations of visitors to exhibitions and museums are known, there seems to be a fairly even balance between information and entertainment, but the entertainment aspect is now gaining in importance. The behaviour of visitors has also been called – in the best sense – "cultural window shopping" (Heiner

Treinen), gazing on the objects representing our art, culture and history. This is not meant in any negative sense, but expresses the museum visitor's need for something culturally stimulating, but "with no obligation", for the museum is now rightly considered to be part of the leisure society.

Serious learning comes from reading. The museum represents a different type of experience, here the exhibits are "vestiges" of history set out on display. Their physical environment acts to some extent as a metaphor for a historic situation and is intended to stimulate visual learning. "Visitors browse like sheep through the landscape of exhibits. We cannot be sure that they read systematically", as the well-known exhibition organiser Ralph Appelbaum put it. This means that the content of the exhibition should not be overburdened with texts likely to strain the visitor's eyes, feet and patience. Visitor-friendly texts should make a favourable visual impression, provide help with orientation, and introduce and complement the displays.

Anyone who observes the behaviour of museum visitors can see that the time spent before each object is very short. For this reason the exhibits need to be chosen with care. What are the criteria for this choice?

Attracting power: the exhibit must attract the visitor's attention.

Holding power: visitors must be able to decipher the "signs" emanating from the exhibit. It is thus a matter of integrating the object and the visitor's particular horizon in an associative or narrative framework.

Communicating power: visitors must be able to use structural and terminological concepts stemming from their particular background to "read" and understand the exhibits in appropriate fashion. Audiovisual aids can be used to place the object – whether isolated or part of a "scene" – in its context, thus allowing it to communicate its "message". This is how the process of communication specific to the museum is engaged.

These three terms – attracting power, holding power and communicating power – were coined by the American museum psychologist Harris Shettel. They succinctly and precisely describe wherein resides the magical power of an exhibit.

Increased knowledge through a visit to a museum is to be expected in particular when two conditions are fulfilled: a basis of individual structural knowledge is present before the visit and there is an active personal interest in a particular aspect of the historical museum's many offerings.

The aim of a good exhibition must be to encourage visitors to engage in dialogue and reflection on history – and above all the present. Forms of communication about it are as important to a good exhibition as the choice of exhibits and the organisation of the exhibition itself.

Asking what visitors can learn about the foundations of the present in a historical museum is an oversimplification. Macro-historical developments are by nature complex and open to interpretation. Experienced history is no exception. As a result, any naive interpretation of history is likely to be excessively simplistic and thus to deform the truth.

Museums and exhibitions can inform and entertain, stimulate discussion, raise awareness of problems, broaden or correct ideas, encourage questions and lead to informed understanding. They thus facilitate the development of a critical and informed citizenship. Present day exhibitions are judged less on whether they faithfully reflect social reality than on whether they are "places of permanent conference" (Joseph Beuys). They thus provide an opportunity for debate, preserving open societies from becoming too complacent, as demanded by the communications theoretician

Neil Postman. A person trained in historical reflection is much more capable of analysing present and future complexities than one who is not.

When thinking of the historical object, the fascination of the authentic comes immediately to mind. Herein lies the difference between the museum and the media. Would a young visitor to a museum be any less fascinated when faced with Adenauer's staff-car – the Gaggomobile – or, to give another example, the train carriage used by Willy Brandt in 1970 to journey to Erfurt than by Napoleon's camel or such treasures as the emperor's crown or the Mona Lisa?

Museums of contemporary history would appear particularly suited to incarnate modern museum design. The historical proximity of their subject matter and the "triviality" of the exhibits, sometimes thought to be a disadvantage or to diminish their attraction, are in fact advantages from the standpoint of communication. The possibility of being able to relive personal experiences and realistically compare past living conditions with those of today, the possibility of forming a positive or negative identification thanks to the immediately evident connections between present and past – all these are communicative processes which are particularly present in the museum of contemporary history.

The "staging" of naturalistic scenes and using forms of organisation which constitute an experience are ways of bringing an exhibition to life. User-friendly services, well-targeted pedagogic programmes and individual guide systems help ensure that visitors are neither out of their depth nor bored. A precondition for such a visitor-oriented approach is to determine the socio-demographic profile of the future visitors. It is necessary to know what they are interested in, their levels of knowledge and their expectations. An open and inviting museum building can attract to the exhibition people who had not planned to visit a museum as part of their look around the town. The museum as a provider of information and entertainment, and also as a forum for the experimental representation of history, can perfectly well occupy a position in public and cultural life no less attractive than that of the theatre, the political cabaret or the amusement park.

The *Haus der Geschichte* aspires to promote an understanding of the principles and operating machinery of the democratic state. It wants to provide information about the broad lines of German post-war history, but above all, it wants to encourage independent reflection on the history of our country. Different levels of information make appropriate communication possible with both the visitor in a hurry and one with plenty of time, with the visitor well-versed in history and one with little knowledge of the subject, with young people and the elderly.

Conclusion: history as a tool for progress, democracy, human rights and solidarity

"Is it possible to teach a historical method without content? To initiate someone in history without any preconceived ideas? Is there a basic minimum? If so, what is it? What is the prerequisite for a critical approach? Is it possible to define a European framework for history teaching (such as relevance of the context; importance of sources; diversity of points of view; effect of selection and conditioning)? To what extent is this approach applied in Europe?" These questions, which were asked at the Paris Colloquy, have guided our thinking about history teaching.

Historians know that history is necessarily biased, but the public is generally unaware of this and is usually credulous. The main aim of history teaching and learning is to show young people that there is no perfect version and that history cannot be approached like mathematics.

It is important to correct the perversions of earlier education systems that are still all too apparent in our present systems.

Schools should pay greater attention to preparation for history learning than to the teaching of historical facts: in the case of history, the emphasis should be on teaching how to learn rather than on imparting facts. Here are some simple exercises for developing historical criticism: how can we ascertain our date of birth? From what point of view are data presented (importance of witnesses and role of the context)? There is also the problem of anachronisms as well as the mistake of presenting the past as if it were the present.

History has a key political role to play in contemporary Europe. It can foster understanding, tolerance and trust between individuals and between the peoples of Europe. It can also be a factor for division, violence and intolerance. Knowledge of history is of paramount importance for civic life: without it, we are much more vulnerable to manipulation, whether political or otherwise.

Appendix

Recommendation 1283[1]
on history and the learning of history in Europe

1. People have a right to their past, just as they have a right to disown it. History is one of several ways of retrieving this past and creating a cultural identity. It is also a gateway to the experiences and richness of the past and of other cultures. It is a discipline concerned with the development of a critical approach to information and of controlled imagination.

2. History also has a key political role to play in today's Europe. It can contribute to greater understanding, tolerance and confidence between individuals and between the peoples of Europe – or it can become a force for division, violence and intolerance.

3. Historical awareness is an important civic skill. Without it the individual is more vulnerable to political and other manipulation.

4. For most young people, history begins in school. This should not simply be the learning by heart of haphazard historical facts; it should be an initiation into how historical knowledge is arrived at, a matter of developing the critical mind and the development of a democratic, tolerant and responsible civic attitude.

5. Schools are not the sole source of historical information and opinion. Other sources include the mass media, films, literature and tourism. Influence is also exercised by the family, peer groups, local and national communities, and by religious and political circles.

------

1. *Assembly debate* on 22 January 1996 (1st Sitting) (see Doc. 7446, report of the Committee on Culture and Education, rapporteur: Mr de Puig).
Text adopted by the Assembly on 22 January 1996 (1st Sitting).

6. The new communication technologies (CD-I, CD-ROM, Internet, virtual reality, etc.) are gradually extending the range and impact of historical subjects.

7. A distinction may be made between several forms of history: tradition, memories and analytical history. Facts are selected on the basis of different criteria in each. And these various forms of history play different roles.

8. Politicians have their own interpretations of history, and some are tempted to manipulate it. Virtually all political systems have used history for their own ends and have imposed both their version of historical facts and their definition of the good and bad figures of history.

9. Even if their constant aim may be to get as close to objectivity as possible, historians are also well aware of the essential subjectivity of history and of the various ways in which it can be reconstructed and interpreted.

10. Citizens have a right to learn history that has not been manipulated. The state should uphold this right and encourage an appropriate scientific approach, without religious or political bias, in all that is taught.

11. Teachers and research workers should be in close contact to assure the continued updating and renewal of the content of history teaching. It is important that history keep pace with the present.

12. There should also be transparency between those working in all areas of history, whether in the school classroom, television studio or university library.

13. Particular attention should be given to the problems in central and eastern Europe which has suffered from the manipulation of history up to recent times and continues in certain cases to be subject to political censorship.

14. The Assembly recommends that the Committee of Ministers encourage the teaching of history in Europe with regard to the following proposals:

i. historical awareness should be an essential part of the education of all young people. The teaching of history should enable pupils to acquire critical thinking skills to analyse and interpret information effectively and responsibly, to recognise the complexity of issues and to appreciate cultural diversity. Stereotypes should be identified and any other distortions based on national, racial, religious or other prejudice;

ii.   the subject matter of history teaching should be very open. It should include all aspects of societies (social and cultural history as well as political). The role of women should be given proper recognition. Local and national (but not nationalist) history should be taught as well as the history of minorities. Controversial, sensitive and tragic events should be balanced by positive mutual influences;

iii.   the history of the whole of Europe, that of the main political and economic events, and the philosophical and cultural movements which have formed the European identity must be included in syllabuses;

iv.   schools should recognise the different ways in which the same subjects are handled in different countries, and this could be developed as a basis for interschool exchanges;

v.   support should be given to the Georg Eckert Institute for International Textbook Research, and Ministries of Education and educational publishers in member states should be asked to ensure that the institute's collection of textbooks be kept up-to-date;

vi.   the different forms of history learning (textbook study, television, project work, museum visits, etc.) should be combined, without exclusive preference to any of them. New information technologies should be fully integrated. Proper educational (and academic) standards must be ensured for the material used;

vii.   greater interaction should be fostered between school and out-of-school influences on young people's appreciation of history, for example by museums (and in particular history museums), cultural routes and tourism in general;

viii. innovatory approaches should be encouraged, as well as continued in-service training, especially with regard to new technologies. An interactive network of history teachers should be encouraged. History should be a priority subject for European teachers' courses organised within the framework of the Council for Cultural Co-operation in-service training programme for teachers;

ix.   co-operation should be encouraged between teachers and historians, for example by means of the Education Committee of the Council for Cultural Co-operation's new project on learning and about teaching the history of Europe in the twentieth century;

x.   government support should be given to the setting up of independent national associations of history teachers. Their active involvement in the European history teachers' association Euroclio should be encouraged;

xi.   a code of practice for history teaching should be drawn up in collaboration with history teachers, as well as a European charter to protect them from political manipulation.

15. The Assembly supports freedom of academic research but would also expect professional responsibility as in the parallel field of broadcasting. The Assembly therefore recommends that the Committee of Ministers:

i.   ask governments to assure continued financial support for historical research and the work of multilateral and bilateral commissions on contemporary history;

ii.   promote co-operation between historians so as to help encourage the development of more open and more tolerant attitudes in Europe by taking account of different experiences and opinions;

iii.   ensure that the right of historians to freedom of expression is protected.

16. European collaboration should be encouraged in the field of history. The Assembly recommends that the Committee of Ministers:

i.   study the basic elements of the different histories of the peoples of Europe which, when accepted by everyone, could be included in all European history textbooks;

ii.   consider the possibility of establishing in member states an on-line library of history;

iii.   encourage member states to establish national history museums on the lines of the German "House of History" in Bonn;

iv.   promote multilateral and bilateral projects on history and history teaching and in particular regional projects between neighbouring countries.

Select Council of Europe bibliography

Against bias and prejudice: recommendations adopted at Council of Europe conferences and symposia on history teaching and history textbooks (1953-95), (doc.CC-ED/HIST (95) 3 rev.).

Teaching history in the new Europe, John Slater, Cassell, London, 1995.

History teaching and European awareness, report of the symposium held in Delphi , Greece, (11-14 May 1994) (doc. CC-ED/HIST (94) 29).

History, democratic values and tolerance in Europe: the experience of countries in democratic transition, report of the symposium held in Sofia, Bulgaria, (19-22 October 1994) (doc. CC-ED/HIST (95) 9).

The reform of history teaching in schools in European countries in democratic transition, report of the seminar held in Graz, Austria (27 November-1 December 1994)(doc. CC-ED/HIST (95) 2).

The European content of the school history curriculum, study by Robert Stradling (doc. CC-ED/HIST (95) 1).

Mutual understanding and the teaching of European history: challenges, problems and approaches, report of the symposium held in Prague, Czech Republic (28 October 1995) (doc. CC-ED/HIST (95)16).

The preparation and publication of new history textbooks for schools in European countries in democratic transition, report of the seminar held in Warsaw, Poland (14-16 November 1996) (doc.CC-ED/HIST (97) 2).

History teaching and the promotion of democratic values and tolerance: a handbook for teachers, Carmel Gallagher (doc. CC-ED/HIST (96) 1).

History without frontiers: a practical guide to international history projects in schools in Europe, Sean Lang (doc. CC-ED/HIST (96) 2).

This publication is based on texts drawn up for the colloquy on "The learning of history in Europe", organised by the Committee on Culture and Education in Paris, in December 1994.

In the same series

Mediterranean strategies (1995)
ISBN 92-871-2667-4

Bridging the gap: the social aspects of the new democracies
(1995) ISBN 92-871-2739-5

The gender perspective (1995)
ISBN 92-871-2822-7

Asylum (1995)
ISBN 92-871-2902-9

The child as citizen (1995)
ISBN 92-871-2994-0

Sales agents for publications of the Council of Europe
Agents de vente des publications du Conseil de l'Europe